"With insight, perspective, and practicality, Dawn Scott Jones helps husbands tackle the difficult and often unaddressed issue of sexual abuse and walk the road of healing beside the woman they love. Dawn's pastoral ministry and personal experience have uniquely equipped her to write a difficult book on a difficult topic. She writes with honesty, candor, and wisdom, offering true hope for healing and restoration. A book that should be in every church library, pastor's office, counseling office, and retreat center, and used as a resource for men's ministries."

—Shelly Beach, Christy Award–winning author of seven books, including *The Silent Seduction of Self-Talk*, and contributor to *The NIV Stewardship Study Bible*

"Packed full of important and powerful truth, Dawn Jones's book is an indispensable guide for the man committed to loving a woman who is a survivor of sexual abuse. For him, this realistic yet ultimately hopeful book will be a lifeline. And for the woman he loves, this is the most profound gift imaginable."

—Steve Siler, founder and director, Music for the Soul

WHEN A WOMAN YOU LOVE WAS ABUSED

*A Husband's Guide to Helping Her
Overcome Childhood Sexual Molestation*

DAWN SCOTT JONES

Kregel
Publications

When a Woman You Love Was Abused: A Husband's Guide to Helping Her Overcome Childhood Sexual Molestation

Published by Kregel Publications, a division of Kregel, Inc., P.O. Box 2607, Grand Rapids, MI 49501.

Published in association with the literary agency of Credo Communications in Grand Rapids, Michigan, www.credocommunications.net.

All websites and phone numbers listed herein are accurate at the time of publication but may change in the future or cease to exist. Groups, organizations, websites, and resources are mentioned for informational purposes and their inclusion herein does not imply publisher endorsement of their activities or contents.

Though the stories of childhood sexual abuse shared here are real, some are composites from women who shared similar experiences. In all instances, beyond immediate family whose permission I have to share their stories, names have been changed to protect the women's privacy.

The author and publisher are not engaged in rendering medical or psychological services, and this book is not intended as a guide to diagnose or treat medical or psychological problems. If the reader requires medical, psychological, or other expert assistance, please seek the services of your own physician or certified counselor.

Library of Congress Cataloging-in-Publication Data
Jones, Dawn Scott.
    When a woman you love was abused : a husband's guide to helping her overcome childhood sexual molestation / Dawn Scott Jones.
        p.   cm.
1. Adult child sexual abuse victims—Rehabilitation. 2. Adult child sexual abuse victims—Family relationships. 3. Wives—Mental health. 4. Wives—Counseling of. 5. Married people—Psychology. I. Title.
RC569.5.A28J66 2012   616.85'8369—dc23   2012018974

Printed in the United States of America

12 13 14 15 16 / 5 4 3 2 1

To my best friends, my sisters, Denise and Debbie

— Contents —

Part 3. How You Can Help

by CECIL MURPHEY

If you're a man and you know or suspect that a woman you love was abused, she needs you. She hurts because someone sexually molested her; you hurt because you love her and sense her heartache.

In her past she trusted someone who took advantage of her innocence and her youth. Nothing can undo that. You're not the one who robbed her of joy and peace—and she knows that. Even so, it may be difficult for her to trust you and to allow you to get too close. She may not be able to ask for help; she may seem to resent anything you say.

In response to her pain, she lashes out at you as if you're the culprit.

Be patient. And read this book.

＊　＊　＊

Dawn Jones is a survivor, and her journey would have been easier if someone early in her life had understood and been able to listen and comfort her. This isn't to blame anyone, because even if someone had asked Dawn, "What do you want from me?" she probably wouldn't have been able to articulate her need.

Until now.

And as Dawn speaks for herself, she also speaks for thousands of others who have been unable to stand up for themselves. Like countless other victims of assault, she felt alone, unlovable, and abandoned.

I understand—at least as much as someone else can. I understand because I'm a survivor of sexual assault. When I finally faced my abuse, I was among the fortunate survivors. My wife, whom I refer to as a cradle Christian, had never been exposed to anything of that nature. When I paused the first night after confronting my past, she said, "I don't understand, but I'm with you."

And she was. And that's all I wanted—for her to be with me. I needed to talk, to feel my own pain, and to explore the dark secrets of my heart. I needed to know that someone cared enough to listen, even if I told the same account a dozen times.

It wasn't easy for Shirley to listen to my litany of sexual and physical abuse. Sometimes she cried; mostly, she held my hand and let me cry.

But she was there.

And you are there for someone you love.

That makes you special—you're the person who can support a woman who needs strong arms, an available shoulder, and a compassionate heart.

You can make the remarkable difference in her life.

SHE NEEDS YOU

I faced most of my healing alone, without the help or encouragement of my husband. I felt isolated and rejected. I kept my feelings to myself, my fears out of sight.

He didn't know how to help me, and even if he wanted to, I didn't know how to let him in.

Right now you may not be sure what to do or how to help the woman you love. And she's not sure either. You may be afraid you might do something wrong and hurt her more. She may be afraid to let you in. It's a confusing time for both of you, frustrating and overwhelming. At times, she may think she can handle her abuse issues alone, at other times she becomes needy and clingy and wants your support. You, the helper, wish you knew how to read her signals better. "When do I give her space?" "When do I try to reach out and help her?"

It would've been so much easier for me to face my abusive past if my husband and I could have created a partnership—if I could have trusted him with my pain, and if he could have learned how to support me.

Helping a sexual abuse survivor overcome the pain of their past is challenging, and most men become confused about how to help.

Understanding the Goal

I want you to know how important *you* are—how desperately she needs your help and understanding—even when she makes it hard for you to believe it's true, even when she treats you as if you're the enemy or the one who hurt her. Your role is crucial, and with your support she can gain victories in areas that she can't achieve alone.

Sexual abuse victimized her, but she made it out. She's a survivor, on her way to wholeness. And you'd like to be one, too—a survivor. You've also been victimized. Her painful past wounds you, too. It's rocked your world, hurt your relationship, and disrupted your life. Now it's time for both of you to come through as victorious survivors.

Your love and support will promote her healing as you journey together. But you also want to protect yourself along the way. You can do that by becoming equipped—the first right step in survival. You'll need to learn how to support an abuse survivor if you're going to have a positive role in her healing process. Helping her, however, can be a daunting task. Without a basic understanding of abuse aftermath to serve as your road-map, you'll most likely fall prey to the exhaustion of the journey.

She turns to you for help, but she may also *turn on you* as she's struggling. I understand that kind of behavior. I hurled my share of verbal darts at my former husband Terry in angry rages. I didn't set out to attack him, but I was triggered by things he said or did and fiercely reacted.

You may have experienced that, too.

At times she hurts you. It can feel that the missiles being launched your way are aimed with precision—designed for deflating you and penetrating your soul. That's her unconscious defense system. It's saying, "You're getting too close to the pain, and I have to make you stop." She probably isn't aware that her reaction is defensive and angry or why she's feeling such strong emotions, but either way, you end up getting hurt. In return, you retaliate and become defensive.

The pattern will continue until you both decide to learn about the process of what's happening and how to effectively diffuse it. Without that knowledge, the cycle of hostility will continue and almost always escalate.

Understanding the Contradictions

Because you love her, you want to understand her, and understanding will take you a long way. But you also want to add mega-doses of other things such as patience, compassion, wisdom, determination, and humor. Some days she'll want to snuggle close and feel your arms around her, and some days she'll strike out at you in anger and cry, "Don't touch me." Understanding abuse will help you develop emotionally thick skin so you can absorb the offense.

It's easy to get lost in the recovery maze and lose hope, so you also need to know your limits. When you're stretched, worn-out, and feel empty, it's time to create a quiet space for yourself. Take a breath and adjust your perspective so you can continue to play a positive role in her healing process.

I use the word *process* because that's exactly what it is—a progression of steps that bring her closer to the goal of wholeness. Her healing won't be quick or easy. For most of us, the process takes years, with small victories along the way. She needs you to help her reach those victories and to celebrate with her each time she conquers another mountain.

You'll also need a realistic awareness of how deeply sexual abuse scars its victims and how involved the journey to wholeness can be. The results of molestation are insidious: they often go unaddressed, and their effects can be cumulative, destructive, and often attributed to other causes. At times her actions may seem unreasonable or strange. She may not cry over a sad event, but lash out over the slightest misunderstanding. She doesn't want to be emotionally disconnected, cold or harsh, but she learned these coping techniques as a child.

You're in her life for love and support, and if you're willing to stay at her side, your encouragement and commitment can help her find the courage to discard old habits that protected her.

Helping a survivor can be—and probably will be—a turbulent process, wrought with confusion and discouragement. Your life will also be filled with contradictions. Just when you feel you've figured out what makes her happy and what's helpful, the rules of engagement change. She laughs at your humor but can turn and snap at you for being insensitive. She's strong and independent, yet can be needy and incapable.

One man said, "I feel like I'm playing in a hockey game, but every time I skate out on the ice, the rules change and I end up in the penalty box, but first I get a blow to the gut."

Survivors aren't really making rules; they're just living by what feels right for them in that moment. Living with a survivor of sexual abuse is a blurry world of uncertainties and double standards. What seemed true yesterday may not be true today. What's permissible for her isn't for you.

Martha, an incest survivor, demanded that she be spoken to in a soft and gentle voice. Since her abuse had also included verbal lashings, she empowered herself by exiting any situation where the discussion became loud and threatening. This made sense to Steve, her partner, and he tried to abide by the keep-your-voice-down rule. Yet whenever Martha became upset or irritated, she raged at Steve, screaming and using profanities.

"I'm confused and exhausted," Steve admitted. "I just can't figure her out."

Martha was unaware of her inconsistency, but Steve felt like she had implemented a double standard. She wasn't giving Steve the same respect she was demanding.

If this dichotomous life is true with you, it means that some days you'll be her hero, and on other days you'll be her enemy. You think you're on the same side, yet she withdraws and treats you as if you're the one who molested her.

One survivor I met named Sherry shared this story about her stepfather, who molested her:

I can still hear his feet shuffling down the hallway heading for my room. When he got close to my bed, I could see his baggy white socks drooping around his ankles. I squeezed my eyes shut in hopes that he would go away. He never did. And neither has the mental image of his disgusting socks. When Tim [her husband] came toward me the other night wearing baggy white socks, I pushed him away and screamed, "Stop it!" I was enraged. Poor Tim had no idea what happened.

At the time, Sherry didn't realize what had happened, and neither did Tim, but she was triggered by a memory. Instead of welcoming Tim's hug—the response Tim was accustomed to—Sherry was hurled into a flashback that elicited disgust and anger. She rejected Tim by pushing him away, a response of disgust she felt toward her abuser.

In similar ways, you may experience frustrating contradictions with the one you love. Try to be patient. In spite of the conflicting emotions pouring out of her, she needs you. She wants you to hold her hand and walk the path of healing beside her.

The journey is difficult. It's maddening. It's exhausting. And it's arduous. But you'll find reward and fulfillment as you experience the beautiful transformation together.

— *Part 1* —

UNDERSTANDING THE SURVIVOR

— *1* —

HER STORY IS UNIQUE

"Will I always feel this shame? I want to be all that my husband needs but I can't seem to trust enough to let him in. More shame. Will I ever escape it?" —Donna

Sexual abuse is one of the most devastating traumas a person can experience. A survivor's life is often scarred in ways that go beyond comprehension.

Perhaps you've seen it.

You're in a relationship with a woman who has been wounded by sexual assault. You want to help her, but you're not sure how. Most husbands struggle knowing how to help, too.

Please keep in mind as you read through these pages, that my words, opinions, and advice are exactly that—mine. The things I've undergone, learned, and witnessed I share from my personal experience. The woman you love has her own feelings, thoughts, and opinions. Although countless women share the identical symptoms and emotions, we are all still unique. Your loved one may not see things from my perspective. Give her the freedom to differ from me and share how her experience feels for her.

My Story

I'm a survivor of childhood sexual abuse. I want to tell my story because I'm hopeful that you'll be able to draw from the insights I've gained and find comfort in knowing that you and the woman you love aren't alone.

Looking back, I can see how ill prepared I was to recognize and process the effects of my abuse. I had no one to help me discover the connection between the deep shame and guilt I felt and the sexual abuse against me. As a result, those emotions continued to grow inside me for years.

I want to tell my story so that others who know this pain can be empowered and get help—both the survivor and you, the support person in her life.

◆　◆　◆

I don't have total recall; however, I have vivid memories that remind me with certainty that I was sexually molested as a child. I can't tell you when it began or how many years it lasted. Until a few years ago, I couldn't have told you how the abuse affected me.

But I can tell you who he was.

Most of my childhood was happy. As the youngest of three daughters, I felt safe, accepted, and loved. I remember lots of laughter and playfulness. My parents were cool—not the overly strict, authoritative parents many of my friends had. My mom and dad were successful and hip, with a relational approach to parenting. Most of my friends would tease by saying, "I love your family. I want to be adopted!"

I found out at an early age I possessed a love for entertaining. It was easy for me to make my family laugh, and that ignited my passion: acting. Standing as the center of attention, I performed skits and acted like silly characters. I even pretended I was filming TV commercials, selling "amazing products with break-through technology." In short, I was a ham who loved the limelight and making people laugh.

I was a happy kid, free and innocent.

I'm thankful for those formative years. That backdrop of love gave me positive self-esteem and a steady foundation to build my life on. Yet behind the curtain of security, the drape of love and protection, lurked a monster—a sexual predator. Bit-by-bit the curtain was pulled back until finally I was forced to face the hard truth.

That sexual predator was my dad by day and my abuser by night.

As I said above, I don't remember the first time he sexually assaulted me, how it started, or how old I was. I only have pieces of jumbled memories. One night I went to bed with the innocence of a child, and the next morning I awakened with intense shame. My father, my childhood hero, had become my abuser. The one I looked to for protection, security, and love had stolen those things from me. My sense of worth was shattered. *Is this all I'm made for?* The question often haunted me. I felt lost, powerless, and ashamed.

Although I can't recall that first experience, other memories are all too clear. I remember one distinctly.

My dad entered my room. I smelled alcohol on his breath as he crawled into my twin bed. As always, I froze. His hands came over me as he stroked my body. My only defense against him was to pretend to be asleep and act like I was completely unaware. To acknowledge his presence was too horrifying to consider.

Thoughts and fears overwhelmed me. Questions flooded my mind.

Why are you doing this? What have I done to make you think this is okay? Stop it! Where's my mom? Does she know what you're doing to me?

In spite of the questions that pounded through my head, I froze and became lifeless. I pretended to be asleep. But I always wondered if asking even one question out loud might have been enough of a deterrent to make him stop.

Don't move and maybe he'll go away. Don't even breathe.

I lay motionless, bewildered, until his fondling was finally over and he crept back out of my room the way he came in. I lay there until I heard the door close.

It's over. You can move now.

But I couldn't move. I couldn't cry. I couldn't feel.

Unveiling Shame

I'd heard of *fight or flight.* When we perceive a significant personal threat, our bodies get ready for either a fight to the death or a desperate flight. But I hadn't heard of the other alternative, which is to *freeze or please.*

I froze.

As an adult, I struggled with my response to the sexual assault against me. I often wondered why I didn't do anything when it happened. I tormented myself with questions: *Why didn't I scream for help or yell to make him stop? Why didn't I say no?*

My reaction to being sexually abused added more pain to the deep shame I already felt. Without realizing it, I self-rejected and scolded myself for being a "stupid victim." That shame was cemented in my heart when my then-boyfriend, later to be my husband, asked me the same question, "Why didn't you do something to stop it?" His response wasn't meant to be cruel, he truly didn't understand, but it shamed me and I made an inner vow that day: *Don't bring this up to him again.*

Yes I froze, and it worked for a while. Then one night I was forced to choose the other alternative: I had to please.

My "act" of playing dead was up. My dad was on to me. This night he wouldn't accept a lifeless contribution. He wanted more; he wanted my engagement. I was terrified. This was new territory. How could I remain innocent and become a participant at the same time? I was perplexed—deeply conflicted. *You want to be an actress,* I thought. *Just do what you have to do and get it over with.* The smell of alcohol on his breath was familiar, and in a peculiar way, soothing. I figured he wouldn't remember this episode anyway; it was another lie I told myself to help me maintain a relationship with him. *Dad never remembers what he's done.* Or, *He doesn't mean to hurt me, he's just drunk.*

I was young and afraid. I had no idea what to do.

"I want to teach you what to do so that someday you'll be able to do this for your husband."

The lesson began, and I was taught where to touch and how to please. I was also taught how to go and get the Kleenex for clean-up. I can't express the deep humiliation that covered me like a blanket. I was bad, stained, damaged, and I knew it.

It's then that I learned both sides of the cycle—freeze or please—and I vacillated between the two.

Freezing and Pleasing

Emotionally, I froze, and stayed that way for quite some time. I was adept at acting as if nothing significant had happened to me. I denied myself any emotional or sexual needs and shamed myself if those feelings arose. This pervasive sense that I was a bad girl for needing something or someone clung to me. One of my journal entries describes it well:

Flawed, damaged, spoiled, ruined. That's how I feel. Prove your worth and perform, or no one will have any use for you. Don't have needs, you'll become a bother. Serve other people—take care of their needs before your own—if you MUST have needs, that is. It's better to try to have none.

I'm not alone in thinking this. Many survivors tend to minimize or dismiss the impact of their abuse by reasoning, "Oh, it's in the past. It's no big deal." Others deny that the sexual abuse took place at all. The pain is too deep and overwhelming to face. When the slightest reminder of her abuse triggers a woman, she's often stricken with anxiety, panic attacks, and depression. These disturbing feelings are usually traumatic enough to send her back into denial.

If a survivor takes the it's-no-big-deal approach to her abuse or ignores it altogether, her denial can mean she's still emotionally frozen and disconnected from her pain. She's not ready to accept the idea of exploring how the sexual exploitation may have affected her, and in truth, is still affecting her.

I denied the thought that I could have further complications from sexual abuse saying, "I've dealt with it, and I'm healed. There's nothing more to talk about." I was terrified to consider the residue of sexual abuse and how it had harmed me.

The woman you love may be terrified, too. She may share the same fear that many survivors harbor. *If I allow myself to feel, relive, or experience this pain, I will completely unravel and become incapable of handling life.*

I gave myself no compassion, but I gave it to others. I understood they had needs, and I believed those needs should be met. I learned to be a people-pleaser. My boundaries were so blurred that I was often confused about what a healthy relationship should look like.

Do I have to meet all of your sexual needs at any time you demand it?

Can I say no to you and still be accepted?

Do I dare let you know I have a need, or will you reject me?

Only years later did I recognize that freezing and pleasing was a pattern I learned as a result of my sexual abuse. I teetered between the two extremes. I was either a doormat or a porcupine. I lost my "voice," my identity in the abuse. My healing journey still includes learning to love myself and be authentic with my needs and opinions.

✦   ✦   ✦

This has been my journey. The woman you love has created her own responses to her abuse. They may be similar or different, but on some unconscious level she has chosen a method of coping—a method that felt safe to her. As a child it's doubtful she trusted enough to share her experience, and therefore no one validated her and assured her of her self-worth. Regardless of how she coped, she's a survivor, and she needs understanding.

WHEN INNOCENCE IS STOLEN

"I sat frozen and unable to think. It was surreal, really. I remember deep sadness; I knew I would never be the same." —Sara

A grandfather takes his granddaughter on his lap and fondles her. A babysitter initiates a game of "Simon Says" and manipulates the child to strip and stand naked. A father reaches into his daughter's shirt to feel her developing breasts. A mother insists on bathing her son and washing his genitals. Each of these examples demonstrates the wide-ranging and often unrecognized nature of sexual abuse that often goes unaddressed.

The Physical Reality of Abuse

People often mistakenly believe that sexual abuse, including childhood sexual abuse, is limited to intercourse or penetration, but many forms of sexual abuse exist. Three basic categories include touching, non-touching, and exploitation.

Sexual abuse can be openly violent or covert—under the guise of "This is my way of showing you how I love you." In whatever form it comes, abuse always involves control and manipulation.

Touching includes:
+ Fondling
+ Forcing a child to touch an adult's sexual organs
+ Inappropriate touching, pinching, or tickling

+ Forcing another to kiss or French kiss
+ Forcing another to perform oral or anal sex
+ Using fingers or objects to penetrate a child's vagina or anus
+ Rape

Non-touching includes:
+ Voyeurism—watching a child undress or take a bath
+ Exposure—showing a child an adult's sexual organs
+ Masturbating in front of a child
+ Forcing a child to watch pornography
+ Sexual intercourse in front of a child

Exploitation includes:
+ Taking pictures of a child naked
+ Using a child for pornography
+ Forcing a child into prostitution

Child sexual abuse is a horrific and selfish crime committed against an innocent child by someone older or more powerful. The perpetrator violates the adolescent for sexual stimulation; however, sexual abuse is about abuse, not sex.

I would emphasize the word *selfish* because perpetrators place their interests over the interests of their unsuspecting victims. They show little concern or compassion for their targets. Abusers are selfish because they damage children's sense of value, worth, and dignity for the rest of their lives. One moment of selfish gratification for an abuser equals a lifetime of pain for a growing child.

Sexual abuse is not a crime of lust or passion; it's a violent crime of aggression, power, control, and domination. "I can overpower you and make you do what I want."

Donna's story illustrates this point.

Little Donna hated naps at the daycare home. After lunch, the older children went outside to play, but Donna was sent to the back bedroom to lie down. Mr. Joe, the big man that helped in the daycare, noticed her disdain. He helped soften the blow at naptime: "Don't worry sweetheart, Mr. Joe is here for you." He picked her up, and threw her over his big, burly shoulders. He bounced her into the bedroom and tossed her into bed. Then he sat next to her and told her a story. His voice was soothing—he caressed her hair and told her that she was a sweet and good little girl. "Naps aren't so bad," he whispered. "They're our special time together."

Their ritual continued. Mr. Joe put Donna to bed and each time he did, he snuggled her a little closer. Soon he was getting into bed with her. The caressing of her hair moved to gentle stroking down her body. Soon he touched and fondled her breasts and genitals.

Donna was confused. Her innocent heart enjoyed his soothing voice and soft touches through her hair. To her it felt like love and compassion. But this seemed different—or was it? Donna wasn't sure.

Mr. Joe seemed different, too. He changed and his voice grew stern. "Don't be a bad girl, lie still and behave. If it wasn't for you, we wouldn't have to take naps."

Donna obeyed, but she was bewildered, confused, and frightened.

Mr. Joe used his power to manipulate the child. After he built deep trust and formed a caring relationship with Donna, he exploited her and became abusive.

Molestation of Mind and Soul

When sexual abuse happens, it shatters the child's trust in the abuser—and her ability to trust others. It destroys her feelings of security. Because the abuse is done at the hands of someone older or more powerful and against the child's will, she is left stripped of her boundaries—feeling powerless, vulnerable, and fearful. She's been intimidated—her self-confidence decimated.

In a case like Donna's, Mr. Joe was her special friend. She felt close to him. If Mr. Joe said she was a bad girl, then she must be. A child like Donna is too young to place responsibility where it belongs—on the abuser. She blames and belittles herself.

Regardless of the form of abuse suffered, whether a single experience or a lengthy season, the child experiences a wounding invasion—a molestation of her mind and soul.

Sexual assault cuts deeply, leaving many negative consequences. Survivors have described various struggles:

+ Shame and guilt
+ A sense of worthlessness and damaged self-esteem
+ Fear, anxiety, and panic attacks
+ Sleep disturbances and eating disorders
+ Flashbacks and impaired memory
+ Fear of trust and intimacy
+ Depression and suicidal thoughts

My Husband's Response

Because you care about her and want her to be whole, you want to understand the psychological imprint abuse leaves on its victims. Everyone's experience is different, but no matter what form of sexual abuse she encountered, it left its mark on her. She'll define how devastating the experience was.

My husband didn't understand the severe impact sexual abuse had on me. At first, neither did I. Terry wasn't able to help me, even though I think he wanted to. Because the abuse happened to me, not to him, he wasn't able to grasp the depth of my pain. I wanted him to help me with an emotional load he wasn't able to take on. I wish it had been different.

As I look back on our times together, I remember feeling pressured. I felt he wanted me to exert my will so I'd hurry up and get over the abuse, move on, and never be troubled again. His inability to "solve" my abuse made him impatient. He wanted his words to be helpful—a kick-you-in-the-pants approach—but to me they were cutting.

"Can't you just get over this?" he'd ask. "Accept what's happened and move on with your life."

The words made sense to him. His stoic upbringing had taught him to sweep problems under the rug. His words echoed what others said as well. I wish it would have been possible for me to "just get over it." He felt that since I'd experienced "only molestation and not penetration," as opposed to violent rape, intercourse, or multiple abusers, I should accept it and "let it go."

"I think you're overreacting," he said more than once.

Am I really overreacting? Have I only suffered a minor offense?

His words crushed me, and so did his attitude. So I criticized myself and minimized my experience. *You're weak and incapable of shrugging off a bad experience.*

It's no big deal. Move on.

But I couldn't move on. If the solution was that easy, what was wrong with me? Was I too weak? Defective? Why couldn't I forget my abuse? I must have asked myself that question hundreds of times. I wanted to bury the past or at least ignore it, but it wouldn't go away. I was stuck.

Today I know I wasn't weak. Struggling with the effects of sexual abuse is expected and the rule, not the exception. My past and all its pain were knocking on the door of the emotional closet I'd stuffed them into, and those emotions wanted out. I tried to move on.

I realized opening the door and acknowledging the past were the only way to move on. But instead, I suppressed my pain and emotionally froze again. Because I felt no support, facing the past terrified me. I was too afraid to be vulnerable with Terry—too afraid to be rejected by another person who was supposed to love me. I felt isolated from my husband, my family, and my friends. I had nowhere to turn and no one to talk to.

I was alone.

Those three words expressed my pain. I had no one. I wasn't even sure God was with me. *After all, where was God when I was weeping?*

Yet I longed to continue my healing journey. I decided to brave it alone.

I have to feel this—I need to heal.

It took me two years to form those words in my thoughts and even longer to say them aloud. But once I accepted that I needed to *feel* if I wanted to heal, I repeated the words to myself out loud.

Sexual abuse robbed me of a carefree childhood, and that reality was difficult to face. But I needed to grieve my unresolved sorrow, and I needed to do it for me. I worked at feeling compassion toward myself by thinking kind and gentle thoughts that replaced the voice of my inner-critic who was always scolding me.

But more often than not, I was intolerant of my tender spirit, and whenever it showed signs of breaking through, I treated it with contempt. Although Terry's attitude about my past sexual abuse was impatient, his lack of understanding and support strengthened my emerging "survival spirit."

Sexual abuse is a big deal, I determined. *I will acknowledge that what was done against me was wrong.*

Self-compassion is still a challenge for me. It's easy to slip back into my default system and become harsh and demanding on myself. I have to remember I'm not bad for having needs, and I'm not flawed for wanting love.

✦   ✦   ✦

The one you love has a story too. Sexual abuse, regardless of its nature, has left a horrific impact on her. It scarred her heart.

You can support her by helping her recognize and feel the damage that was done to her. Encourage her to be honest about the pain of her sexual abuse. Her healing is possible, and with your love and help she can explore the depths of her wounds and begin recovery.

— *3* —

THE CIRCUMSTANCES SURROUNDING HER CHILDHOOD ABUSE

"When she told me about her childhood abuse, I was astonished. I assumed it was a rare case—something you only read about. But now that I've learned about her, I see it everywhere. I'm starting to wonder how many women have been abused." —Jack

What percentage of children—both girls and boys—experience some type of sexual abuse before age eighteen? No one knows for sure. Because most sexual abuse victims don't report, accurate statistics are hard to come by. Most experts agree that the numbers we do have are probably low. Generally accepted statistics estimate:

1. One in three girls have encountered sexual abuse. For boys, the statistics are vague. Some estimates reflect numbers as high as one in three boys to one in seven boys encountering sexual abuse or unwanted sexual contact. The generally accepted figure for boys is one in six.
2. Ninety percent of victims know their abuser. Commonly reported abusers are fathers, stepfathers, brothers, uncles, and grandfathers. Other abusers are babysitters, teachers, and neighbors.
3. Abuse victims don't automatically go on to become abusers themselves. In fact, research shows that this cycle happens less than we may have originally thought. About one-third of people who are sexually abused become abusers themselves. Most

survivors do not go on to abuse. Boys will become abusers more often than girls. Usually those who go on to abuse experience other key factors in their home—domestic violence, maternal neglect, or their abuser was a female.

Every person responds uniquely to abuse. Several factors determine the degree of impact the abuse left on the one you love. It's helpful for a support person to understand some of the details of a survivor's abuse.

Her Relationship to Her Abuser

Generally, sexual abuse committed by a stranger does less emotional damage than the same sexual abuse committed at the hands of a parent or a close, trusted authoritative figure. Because of the trust bond a child has with someone she knows, she suffers more profoundly; the aftermath is much more devastating and complex. In addition to the humiliation suffered because of the abuse itself, the emotional and mental abuse that also takes place is multiplied; feelings of confusion, betrayal, fear, anger, and shame are intensified—compounded by the nature of her relationship with the abuser.

Duration and Frequency of Her Abuse

Usually, the longer the abuse continued, the more negatively the survivor is affected.

Because of my repeated abuse, I learned coping skills to survive. Most survivors develop ways to handle the dysfunction of their lives—perhaps not wisely or well, but they work for us.

The longer abuse continues, the more victims rely on defense systems to survive. This makes recovery difficult. The acquired behaviors—appropriate and needed to survive child abuse—are usually no longer needed or suitable in adult life. The problem is, those behaviors become deeply ingrained. Coping skills—as distorted and awkward as they may be—often become second nature.

Be patient with her when you see her reverting to a survival skill developed in childhood. It takes time and security to lay down the weapons of survival and try a new way of living. And you may identify her defense systems before she does. If she's open to your support, you can help her recognize when she's using old coping skills by gently sharing your observations with her. Encourage her by reminding her that today she's not in danger. She's not alone or helpless. She can lay down her weapons of defense. She is safe.

If She Lived in the Home Where Abuse Occurred

Another factor complicates her healing if she lived in the same home as her abuser. Because she lived in a continual state of "vigilant stress," she couldn't afford to let her defenses down or be caught off guard. Her surroundings were too dangerous and threatening.

One of the ways I expressed vigilant stress (and still do sometimes) occurred when I focused on reading or quietly working by myself. When someone walked into the room, I jumped. This is called a startle response. Most people jump or yell when they're surprised. But for survivors, the startle response is acute. She's ready for fight or flight. Some survivors have even been known to throw a punch when they're taken by surprise. The startle response is another symptom of abuse.

But being easily frightened or jumpy is not the core issue. Extreme stress and vigilance can become a way of life. Because I never knew when my bedroom door would open and more abuse would invade my life, I stayed ready—sleeping with one eye open. After a time, and long after the abuse ended, I crashed under the intensity of the stress. I suffered from panic attacks and depression. Many survivors have similar responses as their bodies' way of saying they can't keep up the fight or flight anymore.

If Her Abuser Was a Woman

Our cultural beliefs make it difficult for us to imagine that a woman would sexually assault a child. But it happens, and when it does, the effects are sometimes more devastating than when abuse occurs at the hands of a man. If it's hard for us as a culture to fathom female perpetrators, imagine how mind-boggling it is for the survivor. It's not surprising she often hides her story; the shame and rejection she feels with this form of abuse is immense.

The majority of sexual assault victims were abused by someone they knew, and most often by family members. Therefore, mothers, sisters, aunts, or grandmothers are the most frequent female abusers. This startling reality makes the thought of female perpetrators even more disturbing.

When I talk about women as sexual predators, I frequently receive arguments or rebuttals. The most common response is, "No mother would do such a thing." Yet, statistics show that twenty-five percent of abusers are women. And of those who report being abused by a woman, eighty-six percent say, "No one believed me."[1] Although experts tell us that the mother-child bond is the strongest human bond, some mothers—perhaps wounded by abuse themselves—do abuse.

For several years I facilitated support groups for sexual abuse survivors seeking healing and recovery called O.A.S.I.S., for Overcoming and Surviving in Strength. I recall one group in particular. One member, who I'll call Rhonda, struggled to participate. Each week while the other women expressed grief over abuse from fathers, brothers, and uncles, she sat quietly invisible, except for occasional shifting in her chair.

One night we were exploring the deep shame we felt connected to our abuse. Rhonda broke down, her cries riveting us.

"How could my own mother sexually abuse me? You think you're bad? I must be *really* bad."

Rhonda's words sliced through the air, and then trailed off into soft sobs.

1. Michele Elliott, "Female Sexual Abuse of Children: 'The Ultimate Taboo,'" *Journal of the Royal Society of Medicine* 87 (November 1984); 692, http:www.ncbi.nlm.nih.gov/pmc/articles/PMC1294939/pdf/jrsocmed00079-0063.pdf.

None of us had ever thought of it before—we were ignorant—unaware that a mother would sexually abuse her own daughter. Even in our efforts to extend help to her, Rhonda felt alienated. She reasoned, if all mothers are wired to love and nurture their children, then there must be something really bad about the child whose mother abused her.

It makes sense that Rhonda would think this way, especially in a world that's loaded with myths about mothers. It was easier for her to believe that the abuse was her fault than to admit that the person who was supposed to love and protect her actually harmed her.

The abuse of a mother toward her child defies everything we are taught to believe about maternal instinct. We see mothers as heroines, protecting their children from harm and danger, even laying down their lives for them. Although it shatters our ideology about mothers, evidence supports that some mothers do sexually abuse their children, a reality that is often unexamined. Mother-son incest and mother-daughter incest does exist and is the most devastating of all sexual abuse encounters and difficult to recover from.

The Type of Abuse She Endured

Regardless the form it may take, sexual abuse is a horrific invasion. The child's will is overthrown, her voice silenced, and her body ravaged. Yet many people falsely believe that the "degree" of abuse determines the severity of impact on the survivor. "It is often assumed that touching and fondling of the breasts and genital area is less traumatic than vaginal or rectal penetration, or oral sex. Not only is this assumption untrue, but other forms of non-touching sexual abuse can be equally devastating from the child's point of view."[2]

Connie, a woman I met while I was an associate pastor at a large church, never experienced penetration when she was abused by her father. But his tactics were no less abusive and her pain no less traumatic. "My stomach

---

2. Lynn Heitritter and Jeanette Vought, "Through the Eyes of a Child Victim," in *Helping Victims of Sexual Abuse: A Sensitive, Biblical Guide for Counselors, Victims, and Families* (Minneapolis: Bethany House, 1989), 30.

churned when the final school bell rang. On days he wasn't standing at the corner, I skipped all the way home. But when I saw him waiting for me, I was nauseous and light-headed. I knew we were 'going for a ride.'" Connie endured sporadic sexual molestation from her father, but she agonized daily from physical symptoms of stress and anxiety. Today she suffers from acute panic attacks and post-traumatic stress disorder.

Coercion and manipulation, mind-games and threats from the abuser to the abuse survivor create profound and life-long complications. Violent forceful acts, as well as verbal and physical abuse in combination with sexual abuse, usually increase damaging effects. If objects are used or the sexual abuse is physically painful and torturous, recovery is usually more difficult.

Her Age at the Time of Abuse

A younger child with less understanding of sexuality generally experiences less trauma from abuse. She may be too young to realize this kind of "touching" is wrong. She's unaware of the crime committed against her, so the shame and guilt associated with abuse are often not present or as prevalent. An older child who has come into some sexual awareness is likely to be more psychologically scarred.[3]

The Response She Received When She Told About Her Abuse

A child doesn't tell anyone she's been abused for many reasons. Most survivors have intense fear about telling someone. *What if I get into trouble? If I tell, everyone will hate me. What if no one believes me?* These fears often stem from the lies abusers use to silence the child.

She's most likely also been weighed down with threats from her abuser. "If you tell anyone what you've done, something awful will happen to you and your family."

---

3. Lynn Heitritter and Jeanette Vought, "Through the Eyes of a Child Victim," in *Helping Victims of Sexual Abuse: A Sensitive, Biblical Guide for Counselors, Victims, and Families* (Minneapolis: Bethany House, 1989), 30.

She may also have developed a special bond with the abuser. Although she wants the abuse to stop, she also doesn't want him or her to get into trouble.

But once a survivor does tell of her abuse, the response she receives from others is of utmost importance. If a significant person believes and supports her, their acceptance helps minimize the negative spiritual and psychological effects. Experts state that a compassionate and supportive response is the most important factor in preventing sexual abuse from destroying a child's life. If a survivor reports her sexual abuse, however, and she's blamed, ridiculed, disbelieved, or worst of all, ignored, she's wounded once again. She's often more ravaged emotionally by the sting of that rejection than she is by the sexual assault.

If Her Abuse Was Incest

Sexual activity that takes place between family members is known as incest. Incest in almost all cultures is taboo—a shameful and despicable sexual assault committed against a person's own family. More incest cases are reported in stepfamilies than biological families.

From fondling to intercourse, incest is the most common form of sexual abuse perpetrated against children, yet most incest survivors admit they did not report their abuse at the time. Incest goes unreported for many reasons:

+ The abuse survivor cares about the abuser and is afraid of what will happen to him or her if she tells.
+ The abuse survivor is told that the activity is "normal in families" and everyone's family does the same thing. The child may not realize she's being abused.
+ The abuse survivor is too young to go for help outside the family.
+ The abuser has threatened the child.

Most often the child is deeply connected to the family or the family member and is told that if she tells anyone, she will ruin the family.

Survivors get the message, "If family harmony is disrupted, it will be your fault." For a long time, I believed my father's threat, "If you tell your mother, she'll fall apart."

Other effective lies that abusers use to silence children include:

- "You're special and this is our special secret."
- "It will kill your mother/father."
- "I'll have to leave you, and no one will ever see me again."
- "No one will like you or ever talk to you again."
- "This is my way of showing you how much I love you. Not everyone gets this kind of attention from me."
- "I'm preparing you to handle those teenage boys that are sniffing around you."
- "I'm the parent and you have to obey me."

Because they're threatened and manipulated, children are left, alone and confused, to deal with their secret. While sexual wounding alone is immense, incest adds profound and often permanent psychological injury. One reason for this deep psychological scar is the intense and intermingled emotional bond children have with their abusers. It's not uncommon for children to love and hate their abusers at the same time.

I loved and wanted the acceptance and attention of my father, but I hated him for the way he gave it. I'm not alone.

Most survivors are abused by someone they know, so a loving and trusting relationship often exists before the abuse. Abusers take advantage of children's affections, and some go to great lengths to nurture and strengthen a trusting relationship before they molest the child. This is called "grooming," preparing the child for abuse. When children are abused by someone they love, massive emotional conflict results.

If One or Both Parents Were Substance Abusers or Violent

Children reared in homes where they're exposed to substance abuse or domestic violence experience a higher rate of abuse than children who come from families where these behaviors are not present. Substance abuse and addiction cause impairment and often contribute to violence. Children in homes where violence occurs are physically abused or neglected at a rate 1,500 percent higher than the national average.[4]

Children are placed at risk in several ways.

Intoxicated parents lose their inhibitions and release their sexually abusive behaviors under the influence of substances. I rationalized the sexual molestation from my father by blaming his alcoholism.

Substance-abusing parents neglect their children and fail to protect them from abusive siblings, other family members, or other potentially dangerous situations.

Appropriate roles and boundaries for family members become blurred. Parental inversion results—the child "parents" the adult, making decisions and caretaking for the father and the mother. Because the spouse of an addicted parent is often left with his or her needs unmet, children are used to fill the vacancies. It's not unusual for children to assume duties such as cooking, caring for younger children, and housecleaning. Eventually, the leap to take "care" of a parent's sexual need is made—and sadly, justified by the abusing parent.

The woman in your life has her own story, and the unique circumstances surrounding her abuse-experience all contribute to shape her. The more you know about the details of her past, the better prepared you will be to understand her and to help her.

---

4. Barbara Correy, *The Painful Legacy of Witnessing Domestic Violence,* http://bit.ly /mJiJPh.

— *4* —

EMOTIONS AND THE BEGINNING OF HEALING

"I'm afraid that if I start to cry I'll never be able to stop, or if I start to 'feel' I'll fall into a black hole and never find my way out." —Joanie

Most survivors repress their emotions. When children experience abuse, they're not equipped to interpret or process the intensity of emotions: pain, rage, fear, bewilderment, guilt, shame, or pleasure. Their emotional circuitry becomes overloaded.

To mentally survive, abuse victims shut down their feelings and go emotionally numb. Tragically, children grow up disconnected from their feelings, unable to experience the full spectrum of emotions.

Learning to Feel

As a kid I liked to make people laugh. I used humor to get me through some lonely and painful times. But in my late teen years, I noticed that while I enjoyed making others laugh, I didn't laugh myself—not out loud and not very big. I wondered how it was that while I really enjoyed humor, I'd lost my giggle.

I didn't cry either. I was stubborn; tears made me feel exposed and defenseless, and I wasn't going to let that happen. I couldn't afford to let my guard down. That's when I made the connection: I was emotionally frozen in every way. It wasn't possible to cut off only the painful emotions. I was numb to all feelings, including the fun and exciting ones.

My breakthrough came a few years later. I vividly remember the night my emotions thawed. I was in the process of recovery and attending a support group for sexual abuse survivors. In one session, a woman shared about her abuse, the abandonment of her father, and the rejection she suffered as a result. During the discussion, I felt restless and agitated.

When the group finished, I was the first to leave. But I couldn't contain my erupting emotions. Tears flowed down my cheeks like streams escaping from some hidden reservoir within me. I couldn't stop them, yet I was terrified to release them. When I arrived home, I called my support group leader. "I'm crying—I mean *really* losing it. Am I going to be okay?"

"Yes, Dawn. God is working on your heart tonight. Go ahead and cry. You'll be more than okay, you'll be free."

Her words brought comfort and reassured me that I wasn't going to self-destruct if I felt the pain. The tears cascaded. I was finally in touch with my pain. Scattered memories and emotions were irreversibly connecting as denial shattered. My healing was beginning.

Something beautiful also transpired that night. After the tears flowed, another stream broke forth.

Joy.

And laughter followed, as I put my head back and laughed from my guts. That night, I reclaimed my emotions.

◆ ◆ ◆

Learning to feel is the beginning of healing.

After years living cut-off from their emotions, many adult survivors recognize they've severed their feelings and desire to reconnect. And although they want their emotions back, many women survivors admit that they're afraid to *feel*.

After being numb for so long, we become unaccustomed to the pain of emotions. We suspend our feelings in an attempt to escape them altogether. But time does not diminish the torrent of our grief and suffering. The lapse merely prolongs our pain. We must let the dam break and allow our emotions to come. Still, many survivors fear they're "going crazy" when they're overcome by feelings.

"I'm afraid that if I start to cry, I'll never be able to stop," Joanie once said to me. She'd sought medical help to cope with depression and soon after began therapy to explore how the depression might be linked to unresolved childhood issues.

But she built trust with her counselor, and over time Joanie disclosed her sexual abuse. As she talked, the suppressed emotions rushed to the surface. Because they were so strong and overwhelming, she became petrified to feel them.

Instead of pressing through her fear, Joanie reverted to denial. She began to use alcohol and prescription drugs to escape the torment of emotions. When she couldn't get her hands on her painkillers, she reached for food in an attempt to remain numb: *I don't have what it takes to handle this pain. I just can't face it.*

After a failed suicide attempt, Joanie returned to her counselor in desperation and started to embrace her emotions. She allowed herself to feel, instead of reaching for instant relief and comfort to stifle the emotions, the default coping system of her past.

Like Joanie, all survivors must do the work of embracing their feelings in order to regain fluidity of their emotions. Remind yourself to be patient. Your survivor is working to "thaw out" from her emotionally frozen state, and the work is hard. She may experience a dichotomy of responses: petrified of her feelings, she may look for ways to deaden herself emotionally, while simultaneously longing to identify and release her emotions.

Once the lid of the suppressed emotion comes off her internal Pandora's box, the release of tears, upheavals, outbursts, and overreactions can overwhelm her—and you, her helper. She may privately fear (and you may fear it too) that she's "going crazy." She may feel a loss of control, and for her, a loss of control is often equated with more pain.

But once she faces her feelings and begins to work through them, the intensity of her emotions and their resulting symptoms usually lessens.

Aspects of Anger

Anger is the most challenging survivor emotion.

Survivors are angry. I haven't met one yet that isn't. Many are volatile; they lash out in fury and release their anger on unsuspecting others.

I listened to Mary's story and tried not to look surprised as she shared. "I stood over my husband, frantically waving a butcher knife, screaming 'I hate you!' I was just trying to get his attention. But he looked really scared, and honestly, I was too. I had no idea I was that angry."

Explosions of rage are easy to detect. But not all anger is easy to spot. Anger can also masquerade as indecision and passivity, and an abused woman can live as an emotional "flat-liner" because of unresolved anger.

Some survivors turn their anger on themselves. They mutilate and cut their bodies; they swallow pills and inflict self-harm in various ways. Others suppress their anger and crash into depression. Self-harmful behaviors are expressions of anger, and most survivors vacillate between various self-abusive behaviors.

As children, we lost our voices; this is one reason for our anger. Unable to express ourselves, we felt betrayed, outraged, fearful, and confused— but we had nowhere to turn. We were alone, so we learned to stuff our feelings inside. But feelings don't fade away or dissolve with the passage of time. Eventually those suppressed emotions reach a boiling point and erupt. As one wise therapist put it, "You can only stuff stuff for so long." Eventually anger leaks out.

Survivors' anger also comes from their unmet expectations. Remember, we survivors don't easily express ourselves, so she probably hasn't clearly articulated her desires. But we all have expectations, strong ideas and desires about how things should be and how people should act. When those silent expectations—known to her but unknown to you—aren't met, she erupts in rage.

Anger can also be used as a coping skill. Many women erroneously believe they can protect themselves from future harm by controlling their environment with their anger. They manipulate and dominate their husbands and children, which, in turn, leaves family members with their own anger issues.

Jim said, "When the kids come home from after-school activities, the first thing they do is ask me, 'How's Mom today?' I usually answer by saying, 'Well, you know your mother. Just stay out of her way.' It makes me sad to see what she's doing to our children. Her anger is controlling everyone."

Sometimes a survivor gets stuck in anger because it's the only emotion she can access. When she's afraid, she reacts in anger. When she's lonely, she responds in rage. When she's rejected, she retaliates with fury. When she feels embarrassed, inadequate, or ashamed, she huffs and sputters and makes life miserable for everyone.

Anger is an easy choice for survivors, and we can use it to "cop out." Anger makes survivors feel less vulnerable, but because anger is often a secondary emotion, it can overshadow the core cause beneath. That's why the healing process should include ways for victims to identify what other emotions they're experiencing.

After an angry outburst, I had to learn how to pause and ask myself, "What emotion am I really feeling? What's behind this anger? Is it fear or hurt? Do I feel abandoned or rejected?" As I asked myself those simple questions, I became more authentic as a person and learned about the sources behind my emotions and state of mind instead of covering up what I was experiencing.

◆   ◆   ◆

The woman you're in relationship with is probably angry. Her post-abuse anger is valid, and most survivors grapple with this powerful emotion during their lifetime. Her anger isn't all bad if she's aware of it and ready to deal with it. Feeling anger is a sign that she's not completely numb and dissociated from her pain. But it's not wise for her to get stuck there. She has to learn how to process her anger, how to acknowledge it, feel it, control it, and release it in more constructive ways.

Again, learning to feel is the beginning of healing, and anger is an important emotion for her to uncover in the confusing time of emotional discovery. But if she taps her anger in constructive ways, the energy of righteous anger can bring her further down the healing path.

5

THE EMOTIONAL CARNAGE OF SHAME, GUILT, AND FEAR

"After my wife got 'in touch' with her emotions, I went numb. I can't process any more of her emotional carnage. I'm cut open, but she's the only one bleeding." —Larry

After my final session as the keynote speaker at a women's conference, I offered to pray with any woman who desired to receive ministry. I gave an invitation for the ladies to come forward. Soon the altar area of the church was flooded.

Woman after woman shared the narrative of her life. The vast majority of them had been maliciously abused—verbally, sexually, and physically. Each woman had her own story, but they all had a common thread—the emotional carnage of abuse dominated their lives and the lives of their loved ones. After I was done praying, I quietly slipped into a back room and wept.

Lord, when does it end? How long will they bleed this pain?

Long after perpetrators leave their crimes, survivors are left to deal with the aftermath of abuse. The aftermath extends into a lifetime plagued with symptoms. And because you're close to her, you suffer, too.

Shame and Guilt

Someone once said, "Guilt is when you feel like you've done something wrong. Shame is when you believe you *are* something wrong."

That definition describes the distinctions well. And survivors are filled with feelings of both shame and guilt.

One woman I prayed for couldn't escape feelings of shame. She approached me with her head hanging down as she whispered in my ear, "I'm cursed with shame. I'm a victim of incest. My mother scolds me and tells me I should be ashamed of myself. Doesn't she know? Can't she see? I'm drowning in shame."

She could barely get the words out as she spoke. And many abuse survivors have heard similar words.

"Shame on you, naughty girl. You ought to be ashamed of yourself!"

Children have heard these words and other stinging phrases spoken by mothers, fathers, and teachers. Tragically, for children of sexual abuse, these words echo in their souls throughout their lives. Shame *is on* them, and they *do feel* ashamed.

Shame carries a deep, inner feeling of exposure. An abused woman feels naked to the world. She self-loathes because her identity is damaged. She sees herself as marred and imperfect and blames herself.

Shame says, "I am defective, flawed, a disgrace." More than a fleeting moment of unworthiness or embarrassment, shame is a pervasive and toxic soul-cancer.

When a survivor feels shame—and most of us do at some point—she alienates herself from others and herself by covering her authentic core person. She reasons, "I can't let anyone see who I *really* am because who I really am is unacceptable and bad. If I let you see who I am, you won't like me—I don't even like me." As a result, the shamed-based woman hides her true self by wearing masks and putting up false fronts. In this way, she becomes an alien—virtually unknown spiritually and emotionally—to others, and sadly, an alien to herself.

In his book, *Healing the Shame That Binds You*, John Bradshaw writes that shame "is a deep cut felt primarily from the inside. It divides us from ourselves and from others. In toxic shame, we disown ourselves."[1]

Feelings of shame permeate our self-worth so profoundly that many survivors resort to deviant behaviors trying to cover up wounded feelings. Behind the *bad-girl* or *wild-child* persona lives a hurting girl with a shame identity. Her behavior is a mirror of how she feels about herself and how she assumes that others feel about her and see her.

Guilt also burdens survivors, and differs from shame.

Healthy guilt can be a positive force in our lives. Guilt helps us determine right from wrong. God gifts us with a sensitive conscience that tells us we've committed sin. Guilt tells us we've violated God's law, man's law, or our own personal code of ethics. Instead of driving us to bad behavior like shame does, positive guilt leads us to make things right. We're inspired to make amends where needed, ask for forgiveness, or make restitution. Healthy guilt says, "I've done wrong. I know to do better." Having a guilty conscience means we've done something out of our character, below the quality of person we believe ourselves to be. Guilt shows we possess self-respect.

Misplaced guilt, however, happens when we take on responsibility that's not ours and feel guilty for something we did not do. False guilt ensnares many survivors. Our perpetrator told us his sinful behavior was our fault. He projected guilt and shame on us, and we accepted it. As innocent children, we owned the guilt for partaking in sexual acts we knew were wrong, and we felt responsible. We believe we should have or could have done something to stop our abuse.

Misplaced guilt fuels our sense of shame and we become trapped: we cannot forgive ourselves. As one person said, "I'm living out a lifetime prison sentence for a crime I didn't commit."

Confronting shame and misplaced guilt is an important part of recovery. Until she discovers the truth about her value and assigns

---

1. John Bradshaw, "The Healthy Faces of Shame (HDL Shame)," in *Healing the Shame That Binds You* (Deerfield Beach, Florida: Health Communications, Inc. 1988 Revised 2005), 5.

responsibility for the crime committed against her, the survivor lives her life as a victim, withdrawn and feeling flawed, bad, and unlovable.

Fear

The clock read two in the morning. I was too frightened to move a muscle, and I strained to see in the darkness. My breathing was shallow, slow, controlled, yet my heart pounded. He must have been gone for almost an hour, but I was vigilant. I wasn't taking any chances.

If he stumbles back in my bedroom, I'll be ready.

My resolve was fierce. I spent many nights stabilizing myself after yet another abusive encounter. No wonder that years later I crumbled in exhaustion under the pressure of anxiety.

Trauma survivors learn that the world is a frightening place; bad things happen to blameless children. We also discover that "trusted people" can't be trusted. We fear even more victimization, so we learn to take control.

For most of my childhood, I believed I had to take care of myself to feel safe. But I also felt completely ill-equipped to do so. My helpless feeling created a tremendous amount of anxiety. Later in life that anxiety expressed itself in full-blown panic attacks and random episodes of anxiety. I felt terrorized by a continual sense of impending doom.

Survivors experience anxiety over many things. At first glance our fears may appear to be disconnected, inconsequential phobias. But a better understanding of a survivor's past usually explains their fears.

Let me illustrate. I often teased my high school girlfriend for her bizarre fear of green olives. She said, "They give me the creeps." I snickered at her dislike and tried to convince her to conquer her fear by eating a small olive. But she was genuinely repulsed by them and wouldn't touch one. Later, she revealed to me that during a Christmas vacation at her relative's house, her older cousin had molested her. After his acts of abuse, he stared at her from across the room with a penetrating gaze—intimidating her to assure her silence.

"His eyes burned a hole in me. I'll never forget his piercing green eyes."

Her hatred for green olives instantly made sense.

*   *   *

Women who were sexually assaulted demonstrate classic fears:
- Fear of intimacy
- Fear of the dark or being alone
- Fear of independence or decision-making
- Fear of dependence and vulnerability
- Fear of authority or authority figures
- Fear of people or social situations
- Fear of closed places such as elevators or airplanes
- Fear of leaving the home, traveling away, or going outside
- Fear of driving
- Fear of men
- Fear of sex

Survivors are riddled with shame, guilt, and fears of many kinds after even one sexual abuse experience. Often plagued for a lifetime by these emotions, survivors in the process of recovery must recognize how shame-filled thoughts, guilt-based identities, and fear-driven behaviors control their lives. Once a survivor detects negative emotions, they are another step closer to finding freedom.

6

BEYOND EMOTIONS, FROM LONELINESS TO DEPRESSION

"It bothers me when my wife says she feels completely alone. How can I spend any more time with her than I already do? We're constantly together. Yet there seems to be some impossible-to-fill, Grand Canyon–sized hole in her heart. I don't know what else to do to ease her loneliness." —Joel

At times I felt alone, even though I was surrounded by people. I smiled, played, and clowned around, hoping to make others laugh. But the inner me stayed hidden, masked. And no one seemed to notice.

How could I feel loved and connected when no one knew the real me? I was posing. If they really knew me, would they like me or reject me? Who could I trust? Who would help me? I was only a child and not mature enough to grasp what had happened to me. My father, the man who was supposed to protect me had hurt me. I was different than other girls. I felt alienated and lonely.

Loneliness

The abuse we've suffered makes us feel alone and, indeed, as abuse survivors, we are alone. We hide a powder keg of secrets. Secrecy inherently makes us withdraw and isolate from others.

Some definitions say that *aloneness* is a state of being while *loneliness* is a state of mind. A person can be alone and yet feel content and satisfied. They enjoy their solitude. On the other hand, someone can be sitting in the midst of a crowd of people and feel lonely. *All these people are here and not one of them realizes what I'm going through.* In fact, being with others can increase loneliness. *I'm screaming inside, but no one hears me.* That's how I felt—unheard and ignored.

Survivors often feel intense loneliness. "It gnaws away at my soul," one woman said. "I can't get away from feeling like no one is really there for me. I feel completely alone, caught in my own world of pain." Perhaps the woman you love has battled with loneliness, too. Talking through her abuse issues with someone she trusts can help her resolve much of her loneliness, but it won't solve it completely. She's learned to withdraw and bury her emotional needs, and it will take her time to learn how to open up, express herself, share her needs, and talk about her fears. Until then, it will not be uncommon for her to feel isolated and alone.

Abandonment

The secrecy of sexual abuse creates loneliness for most survivors. We hold back a part of ourselves, which prohibits us from creating deep, authentic relationships. When we do have meaningful relationships, they're difficult to sustain because we remain guarded, fearful of exposure. And we're afraid of exposure because we assume—among other things—that exposure will mean abandonment.

Feelings of abandonment are almost universal for survivors. The feeling stems from the loss of nurture, the lack of belonging, and the absence of love itself. It involves the grief of aloneness-not-by-choice, betrayal, and sadness for the vacancy of a caring, loving, and supportive *someone.*

Abandonment feelings and fears are especially true if the abuse was incest. She not only suffers the loss of relationship with the one who abused her, but with the disclosure of the abuse comes the inevitable loss of other family relationships.

You won't love me anymore if you find out I'm damaged.

Everyone will hate me if talk about it.

The family will be destroyed if I tell, and it will be my fault.

Many survivors carry abandonment issues well into adulthood.

These issues wreak havoc in relationships. Her insecurities usually take their toll on relationships, and her fear of abandonment becomes a self-fulfilling prophecy. The thing she most wants to avoid comes to pass: she's abandoned again. The relationship is destroyed under the demands of her expectations, possessiveness, or the "rejection, don't-leave-me" cycle. Some women develop a pattern of attracting men who will indeed abandon them. And in spite of the destructive nature of abandonment, people are often unaware of how it affects the abuse survivor.

It's possible you've felt the fallout of her abandonment issues. You've wondered why you're tempted to throw up your hands and quit. It's possible she's unknowingly testing you and your commitment to stay by her side. Although she loves you, she pushes you away to discover, *Will he leave me too?*

If this is happening with the woman you love, talk with her. If she's open to talking, take a compassionate look at the issue together.

Depression

I was only a few minutes into my Tuesday morning and already felt drained and overwhelmed. Although I tackle most mornings with enthusiasm, I was slow on the uptake this day.

I felt strangely different.

That Tuesday would be day one of 164 more days just like it. For the first time in my life, I was experiencing depression. And I was in deep.

Survivors frequently experience depression. The emotional and physical symptoms of depression range from feelings of sadness to more severe signs such as overwhelming hopelessness, persistent despair, and feelings of suicide.

✦   ✦   ✦

If the woman you love is experiencing any of these symptoms, she may be exhibiting depression:
   ✦   Loss of enjoyment from the things she once found pleasurable

- Decreased energy and/or motivation
- A feeling of sadness
- Feelings of unworthiness, guilt, and inadequacy
- Appetite or weight changes
- Inability to sleep, restlessness, or waking up feeling tired
- Excessive sleep or feelings of needing more sleep
- Irritability or grouchiness
- Inability to concentrate or make decisions
- Stomachaches and digestive problems
- Headaches or other aches and pains
- Sexual dysfunction
- Death wish or thoughts of suicide

If she's suffering any of these symptoms, it's wise to pay close attention to her. Feelings of sadness can turn into a deeper problem.

Until that morning I had rarely experienced a blue day, and never one that I couldn't bounce back from. But my sadness was more than blue—it was black. When black Tuesday swept in on me, depression came like a terrorist. Despondency captured and paralyzed me. I cried out to God in anguish, "Where are you, God? Why is this happening to me, Lord?" The mental torment was excruciating.

Prolonged and severe episodes of depression should be taken seriously. Survivors do contemplate suicide and even attempt it. If your partner is sinking deeper into despondency, seek professional help right away.

The "Forever" Feeling

Many of us look at the long road of recovery ahead and feel overwhelmed. We wonder if we'll ever be normal, if our lives will ever be free from the pain of the past.

The answer is yes.

Survivors can live free, healthy lives and experience fulfilling, intimate relationships. Healing is a process, but if a woman is committed to the journey, wholeness will come.

Walking through depression (simply crawling some days) was one of the most difficult and terrifying experiences of my life. Paradoxically, this chapter of life was also one of the most faith deepening and rewarding seasons I've ever known. Facing depression motivated me to delve into the mire of my past—the battle I was avoiding—and became the catalyst to my freedom.

— 7 —

HOW HER MEMORIES SURFACE

"My wife was fine for twenty years of our marriage—then suddenly she had a memory from her childhood. Now everything's changed. With one flashback from the past, the wife I knew was gone." —Steve

I don't know when my abuse began, but in the earliest memory I can recall, I was twelve or so. And I'll never forget what happened to me.

I think I may be one of the fortunate ones. I *know* I'm a survivor. Because I remember my abuse, certain things about me make sense. I know why rage rises within me when I view movies or listen to newscasts about innocent children being abused. I'm aware that being "trapped" gives me a feeling of helplessness and physically triggers me. I get knots in my stomach and feel nauseous. I feel twelve again—trapped in my bed, helpless, and without a way to escape.

Memories

Not everyone has memories of their abuse. The actual experience of sexual abuse is so horrifying, so stressful and overwhelming, that it's common for children to push the encounter away from their conscious mind and into the deep recesses of their soul, unremembered for years. It's a child's way of surviving. They disconnect and block out all awareness of abuse in order to function and maintain some facade of normalcy.

Blocking memories can temporarily protect children emotionally, psychologically, relationally, and in many other ways that save them from devastation. Forgetting what happened may protect her for a time, but repressed memories frequently return, often five or ten or even forty years later. Frequently, once a person is well out of danger and feels assured of their safety—either consciously or unconsciously—past, forgotten memories intrude into the present. And when those memories come, they demand attention.

You may ask, "If the memories are buried then why not just leave them there?" The answer is simple: because buried memories still hold power. They have the potential to create gnawing symptoms like anxiety, low self-esteem, depression, chronic pain, interpersonal dysfunction, substance abuse, self-mutilation, and suicidal ideation. Sometimes survivors mistakenly believe that the symptoms are the source of the problem. But symptoms reveal underlying problems: unresolved sexual trauma. Unless the memory is confronted, a woman may continue to act out, not knowing the cause for her depression or anxiety.

One woman I met named Catherine cried in anguish as she shared. Cat, as she liked to be called, was plagued by memories that popped into her mind without warning. She was afraid to close her eyes, afraid to fall asleep at night. Her confusion was revealed by her questions.

"Why now? After all these years, why do I have to face my past now?"

"Why not now?" I countered. "When did you think you were going to deal with your abuse?"

"Why never, of course. At least that's what my counselor told me."

"What?" My face gave me away. I wondered where she could've received such poor advice.

Cat told me the story.

"When I was in my twenties I went to see a counselor. I was experiencing depression, anxiety, and fear. I thought it might be due to my past sexual abuse. But when my therapist asked me what happened, I said I didn't remember most of it."

That's when the counselor told Cat that she had been given a great gift by God: amnesia. Cat should continue to suppress the memories. "Keep them buried and go on." And for the next thirty years that's exactly what she did.

Now, at fifty-two her suppressed and forbidden memories were trying to break through to her conscious mind.

A memory may resurface in many ways. In his book, *When a Man You Love Was Abused*, Cecil Murphey talks about several different types of memories that can occur:

1. *Visual Memories.* Images can be clear or vague and blurry, but distinct enough to cause the woman to remember and sometimes relive the abuse as if it were happening all over again.

2. *Auditory Memories.* A memory can be triggered by sounds: music, heavy breathing, someone whistling, footsteps, a door opening, or other related sounds.

3. *Sensory Memories.* Memories are triggered through certain smells, like toothpaste, alcohol, colognes, or body odor. A woman may freak out when she smells the brand of men's cologne her perpetrator wore.

4. *Body Memories.* Just as an athlete's muscles "remember" because of repetition and training, our bodies retain memories due to reoccurring and repetitive sensations. In the same way that other memories resurface, repressed body memories can occur spontaneously. Some survivors experience pain or sensations flowing over their genitals at unexplained, random times. If she complains of phantom pains in her breasts or genitals, know she's not crazy. Her body is reexperiencing trauma, even though she has no cognitive memory.

5. *Emotional Memories.* It's possible for survivors to experience emotions (feeling sad with no apparent reason) and triggers (reacting to newscasts and other stimuli) but not understand these responses are connected to the sexual trauma of their past. Feeling powerless can trigger memories. When an event

resembles the feeling of being out of control, the survivor can have memories or flashbacks and relive their trauma.

Triggers

A trigger is an outward stimulus or catalyst that causes an emotional or physical reaction. When a survivor is triggered, she often feels disoriented and can have trouble distinguishing the present from the past. Triggers can cause anxiety, startle responses, fear, and other symptoms.

As one survivor put it, "When I'm triggered, I'm instantly catapulted into the past. I emotionally crash to the ground, and there's no mat."

A trigger can be anything—a certain smell, a touch, a sound—and survivors never know when they will come. A woman can be triggered by the smell of alcohol because her abuser was drunk when he attacked her. The nice old man who greets at the church on Sunday mornings smells like Old Spice. She reacts in an instant because Grandpa wore Old Spice and molested her. Another woman bristles when her hairdresser touches her hair. A female relative caressed her hair before she fondled her.

Some women are triggered by certain words. Being told to "relax" triggers me. My abuser used that expression. When I hear it, I involuntarily stiffen up, a far cry from relaxing. Another common verbal trigger for female survivors is the phrase "I love you." Abusers are notorious for using this one. The woman you love may have a hard time hearing you say "I love you," and a harder time understanding what you mean when you say it.

It's important for survivors to understand our triggers. Without that knowledge, we're apt to think, "I don't like my hairdresser, she gives me the creeps." Instead of recognizing our sensitivity, we change hairdressers, churches, and partners. In an effort to stop the pain, survivors run from triggers, when we should look inside for healing.

The goal of therapy is to diffuse the intensity and power of triggers. One way we do that is to identify specific triggers. It's not wise to avoid them altogether, which would be nearly impossible, but to expose ourselves to them little by little so we can learn new responses.

She may need your assurance as she goes through this process. Help her with positive self-talk that says, "I'm okay. I can handle it today. I'm not a helpless child, I'm a healthy adult." You can also support her by helping her evaluate her experience. "What was the trigger? What were you feeling? What can you do for yourself this time that you couldn't do before?" Questions like these can effectively help her safely ride the wave of emotion and fear and in the process diffuse the magnitude of the trigger next time.

The intimate sexual experience is a virtual landmine for triggers. Take time to investigate sexual triggers in her life. Many couples are caught off guard when their evening of candles and romance turns into a chaotic, dark, and stormy night. Without finding and dismantling triggers, your intimate life will remain tempestuous.

Flashbacks

Flashbacks are quick and sudden memories that intrude into our present. They're often produced by a trigger. Flashbacks can be blurry and fuzzy images or clear, dramatic, and precise pictures. These quick flashes abruptly transport the survivor back to the past where she relives or reexperiences her trauma.

Although flashbacks are disruptive and frightening, we who experience them shouldn't fear them. They may be a positive sign that we're moving toward healing. Our psyche is telling us, "I'm ready to recall and process the past." Rather than hastily dismissing scenes from the past, survivors should "flow" with the memory and allow the flashback to sweep over us. Once we understand we're having memory flashbacks of our past, the fearful power of the flashback is diminished.

My flashbacks were never clear; they were more often a sensory memory. I couldn't see any real images, but I had emotions and sensations. The flash could come in an instant and last for only a few seconds, but when it passed over, I was left weak, nauseous, and drenched with perspiration.

At first I wasn't sure what was happening; I described the feeling as a "déjà vu" experience. Something seemed familiar, yet it was vague. I now understand it was a memory trying to push its way to the surface.

One woman in the recovery process said she kept having flashes of what she thought was a blanket coming down on top of her. It covered her face and smothered her. As the flashbacks continued to come, they increased in length and clarity. Finally, she had a clear picture. The blanket was the flannel shirt of the man who molested her. He had laid on her and forced himself into her face. "I couldn't breathe," she told me. "I tried to move, but every time I did, he pushed himself deeper into me." The flashback was painful and the full memory was even more difficult. But once she processed the memory, the flashback stopped and she started healing.

Dissociation

Dissociation is another common response to trauma. When a disruption in the normal psychological function of the conscious mind occurs, allowing the mind to separate itself from experiences that are too overwhelming for the psyche to process, it's known as *splitting off* or *dissociation.*[1]

High levels of dissociative symptoms are found in adult survivors whose child abuse was particularly violent or gruesome. The abuse was too much to bear, and since the child was prohibited from leaving physically during the sexual assault, she left psychologically. This mental escape allowed her to split away from her present, painful circumstance by cutting off all inner thought and awareness of what was going on. Instead, she dissociated; she traveled somewhere pleasant and soothing in her mind.

Children who dissociate unconsciously separate themselves from the pain by storing the memories away into the corner of another room in

---

1. *What Is a Dissociative Disorder?*, Sidran Institute, http://www.sidran.org/sub.cfm?contentID=75&sectionid=4.

their minds, which becomes unavailable to the conscious mind. In other words, they mentally and emotionally check out. This is a powerful survival skill, and the survivor learns that it's a temporary yet effective way of fleeing from sexual abuse.

But like the other coping skills of the survivor, what was acceptable and useful during the sexual ordeal of childhood is not useful in the everyday living of adulthood. This is often where the wounded woman struggles. With dissociation, she learns that when things become intense or emotionally too difficult and stressful for her to handle, she can split away from reality and "numb out." But the dissociative response can happen automatically, even at times when it's not needed or desired. Splitting no longer serves the woman as a protective shield when it prevents her from being "present."

If the woman in your life is experiencing unwanted dissociation or if you suspect she is often dissociating, you'll want to find professional help. Her healing journey will need to include learning how to stay in the present and grounded in reality.

Many survivors' memories begin to surface several years after abuse. When they enter therapy to process their abuse, even more memories are likely to surface. As memories return, it's important that survivors be encouraged to process them with someone they trust. It's not necessary, however, for a survivor to uncover every memory for healing to occur, nor is it wise for them to press themselves to remember. Memories should be allowed to surface gradually and naturally.

— *8* —

MESSAGES SHE HEARS,
LIES SHE BELIEVES

"I tell her I love her all the time. But she just stares at me with scrutiniz-ing eyes. She says she doesn't believe anyone could love her. How can I con-vince her?" —Jon

When a seed falls to the ground, it goes deep into the soil. If it takes root—and it usually does—it produces fruit. Like seeds, words have power to give life. When they're spoken into the impressionable soil of a child's mind, those words, positive or negative, take root and manifest results.

Words alone aren't the only influence that shapes the developing mind of a girl or boy. As we travel through life, we constantly interpret the "messages" we hear. We observe the actions of others and note how they make us feel. We listen to the words they speak, but perhaps more importantly, we hear the inflection of their voices and other nonverbal signs. Eventually, we form beliefs and opinions about ourselves, others, and life through the words and messages sown into our hearts.

Brenda, for instance, was told by her father, "Whatever you do, don't be like your brother." Brenda was four years younger than her brother Steve, but old enough to notice that her brother and father clashed. The two of them frequently argued. Brenda's mother seemed fragile, inca-pable of handling the conflict. To relax, Brenda's mother often drank.

Brenda could recall her stressful feelings at the age of eight, "It felt like everyone was watching me to see if I was going to follow in Steve's footsteps."

Brenda heard a message: "If you want to be accepted, you have to be what we want you to be."

Brenda worked hard at gaining her father's approval. She was compliant and earned his attention. She became a "good little girl" for her mother, doing household chores and making meals. She heard another message: "You're responsible for our happiness."

When Brenda was nine, her father approached her while she was sitting by the swimming pool. He picked her up and threatened to throw her in. He laughed when she pleaded to be put down. Instead, he ignored his daughter's cries and threw her in.

Brenda internalized another message: "I'm not valuable. My feelings don't matter."

It's not a surprise that by the time Brenda was ten, she had formed the belief that her opinions and desires were unimportant. She believed the lie, "I'm not worthy enough to be validated."

Brenda became an easy target when her father entered the bathroom one night. He demanded she undress so he could give her a bath. Brenda thought to protest, but she'd lost her voice a long time ago. She shrank in humiliation when her dad took the soap and lathered up her body, "We have to make sure your private parts are especially clean. Inside and out."

Brenda was conflicted. She loved special attention from her father, but his touch inside her vagina was troubling and deeply confusing.

Brenda learned a new message: "Bad attention is better than no attention."

Driven by the lie that she wasn't worth much, Brenda married young. Not surprisingly, her husband doled out more verbal and physical abuse.

The woman you love believes her share of lies as a result of her sexual trauma. Messages can become so infused into the psyche that she probably isn't always aware of the lies she believes or how powerful they are. In fact, unless survivors develop an intentional desire to discover and dismantle these lies, they will continue to be controlled by them.

Common lies survivors believe are listed below. Maybe you've heard her speak these exact thoughts, but more often, you will detect distorted beliefs as you observe them operating in her life. Because these lies can be so powerful, it's important that you gently help her see the truth and combat each lie.

The Lie She Believes: It was my fault.

This is a big one.

Kids use magical thinking—they believe everything has to do with them and that somehow they're responsible. This is easily observed when children experience their parents' divorces.

It's my fault my mommy and daddy aren't together anymore.

The same holds true with sexual abuse. Children believe "It's my fault."

I was the final presenter at a women's conference this past spring. As is my custom, I invited those who wanted extra ministry to come forward at the end of my message and receive prayer.

One woman named Dorothy got up from her seat and walked to the front. As she came, I heard the words in my heart, *Tell her it's not her fault.* I was taken aback at how clear the impression came. I knew I had to give her the message, but still I worried, *What if I heard it wrong? She'll think I'm crazy.*

But the message was too clear to dismiss.

As we joined hands to pray, I leaned into her ear and whispered, "This may seem strange to you, but I believe God gave me a message for you. He wants you to know, it's not your fault.

Dorothy doubled over, like she had just been punched in the stomach and let out a cry.

She sobbed uncontrollably for several minutes. After a moment, I knelt beside her and asked, "What can I do for you?"

"You have no idea what this means to me. I've carried the guilt of my childhood rape for years. Today, I told God that I needed to know if I was to blame. I can't believe how he answered my prayer."

Then she shouted for all to hear, "It's not my fault. It's not my fault. It's not my fault!"

The Truth: Sexual abuse is never the fault of the child. No matter the circumstances surrounding our experience, we are blameless. The responsibility lies solely on the abuser.

God makes this clear:

> And whoever welcomes a little child like this in my name welcomes me. But if anyone causes one of these little ones who believe in me to sin, it would be better for him to have a large millstone hung around his neck and to be drowned in the depths of the sea. (Matt. 18:5–6)

The Lie She Believes: It felt good, so I must have wanted it.

Survivors struggle with guilt and confusion when they experience sexual pleasure during their abuse. They're deeply troubled and humiliated for being physically stimulated. Many feel their bodies have betrayed them in the worst way.

Most survivors determine not to give their perpetrator the satisfaction of seeing them receive enjoyment from the sexual abuse, but in spite of a rational decision, physical pleasure sometimes occurs during abuse. Perpetrators exploit children even further when they force their victims to reach sexual fulfillment, touching their bodies in ways that arouse sexual feelings. Mental abuse follows when the abuser makes condemning comments such as, "See, you enjoyed this. You really wanted it."

As a result, survivors hate their bodies even more.

The Truth: Due to prolonged sexual stimulus, sometimes a physical response takes place for sexual assault victims; the body reacted as it was designed to and the survivor derived pleasure. But remember, the pleasure was a physical response, manipulated by someone more powerful. The reaction should never be interpreted as emotional, spiritual, or relational enjoyment.

The Lie She Believes: I'm bad.

Flawed, contaminated, defective, and damaged.

These words are used by many survivors to describe themselves. Self-rejection is an intense, reoccurring struggle for them. A woman looks in the mirror and hates what she sees. She despises herself and feels like she doesn't measure up to other girls. Her self-esteem was shattered long before her adult life ever unfolded.

"I can't remember a time when I felt good about myself. I've always hated me."

An elderly woman in our support group lived her entire life with feelings of self-hatred and disgust. Only through the help of support did she begin to find self-worth.

The Truth: God tells us in his Word that we are "fearfully and wonderfully made" (Ps. 139:14). Our very creation was God's delight, and he declared us "wonderful." Life's circumstances hurt and wounded us, but we are not bad and defective. Our identity can be renewed and restored by God's healing power.

The Lie She Believes: No one can love me.

Because of deep-seated shame and self-loathing, wounded women often settle for relationships that are toxic and dysfunctional. They frequently attract men who continue to abuse them. This confirms the lie, *No one will love me.*

After a history of exploitation, this lie—coming from their abuser or from themselves—propels some survivors to accept maltreatment because they're convinced they deserve nothing better.

The Truth: Women are not commodities. Damaged self-esteem has left them feeling as though they're nothing more than sexual objects. But women are inherently valuable; we are not substandard. We are loveable.

The Lie She Believes: I have to be sexual to be loved.

Sex equals love. This is the message many survivors unconsciously believe. We were exploited at a young age, and the attention we received confused us. It felt good to receive affection. Who doesn't enjoy feeling loved and accepted? But at the same time, we were disgusted by the manner in which that affection came. The convoluted conclusion some survivors arrive at is that some attention is better than none at all.

However, when survivors reach adulthood, they have difficulty distinguishing between sex and love. They often believe being loved means having a sexual experience. Identities become tangled. In the minds of survivors, sexuality and worth are connected.

But you can help her by reminding her of God's truth.

The Truth: I'm loveable because God made me. I'm loveable because I'm his priceless creation. I'm also loved because I'm precious and special. I don't have to earn love by performing sexual acts or being sensual. I'm worthy of love.

The Lie She Believes: My abuse wasn't that bad. I'm over it.

Minimizing the impact of abuse or its results is a classic defense mechanism for survivors. It's denial in the most obvious form. A woman in denial makes statements like:

It hurt at the time, but I've gotten over it.
If I act like it didn't hurt me, then it didn't.
If I ignore it, then it will go away.
Don't talk about it; it's buried in the past.

One woman was told she was violating Scripture when she complained about her hurtful past. "The Bible says you have to 'forget what lies behind.' You're not permitted to dig it up."

Forgetting and burying the past doesn't erase it. It doesn't eliminate the negative symptoms that continue to plague survivors.

Sexual abuse has ripped us apart like a hurricane.

To try to live as though debris isn't scattered at our feet is ridiculous. Ruin can't merely be swept under the rug and ignored. I know—I tried it.

I minimized my pain and denied the immensity of the crime inflicted on me. I told myself my abuse was *not that bad,* and discounted the negative symptoms I struggled with as being *no big deal.*

The Truth: Our healing accelerates when we're willing to admit it was horrible. We were violated, humiliated, and disgraced. We have to be willing to break down our walls of denial, become vulnerable, and take an honest look at abuse fallout.

It takes time for a survivor to uncover lies and distorted messages present in their lives as a result of sexual abuse. In fact, most survivors will probably continue to discover twisted beliefs over the course of their lives. But as the woman you love works through her trauma, the light of discovery will slowly seep into the dark places of her mind and illumine lies and false beliefs controlling her thoughts. She will gain freedom as she detects these lies and replaces wrong messages with God's truth.

9

HER DISTORTED SELF-IMAGE

"I try to speak loving and kind words, but by the time she hears them, they've been twisted into 'cruel, heartless, and cutting remarks.' I wish I knew what happened between the time I speak the words and the time they reach her ears." —Cliff

I hate myself. I'm fat and ugly. How can anyone look at me?

Even the most beautiful women believe these things. She looks in the mirror and sees a person she despises. She slides on a pair of size 2 jeans and feels fat.

She believes these misconceptions because her thoughts aren't based in reality.

Like an untamed horse, distortions run wild through the mind of a survivor. The acute psychological wound from sexual assault distorted her thought-filters. If left unchecked, distortions will take over where abuse left off. Assaulting her mind, they will devastate her.

A Blurred View

I am nearsighted. If I remove my contacts or glasses, my vision is so impaired that I can't see two inches in front of me. To say the least, I'm visually challenged. To make matters worse, when it came time to renew my prescription, I found out my eyes had declined even more. My prescription wasn't accurate, and it hadn't been for a long while. I'd been living with decreased vision, and I wasn't seeing as clearly as I thought.

When my new glasses arrived and I put them on for the first time, I was amazed at what I could see. Grass wasn't one solid, green piece of velvet after all, but a sea of individual blades. My imperfect eyesight had distorted the image.

When the mind of a child is corrupted by sexual assault, her perspective is shaded by the lens of the past. She doesn't realize she's not seeing clearly until she's presented with the truth. Even then she may resist. She's seen things through the lens of rejection, fear, or shame for so long that it's difficult to see reality.

Distorted thoughts make us depressed and anxious. Because we confuse what *feels* true with what *is* true, we live defeated lives.

Distorted thinking manifests in many ways.

One way is in *black-and-white thinking*. You can identify this "all or nothing mind-set" by the use of the words *always* and *never*.

"You *always* ignore me. You *never* say anything nice to me."

A second form of distorted thinking is *mind reading*. A woman is likely to jump to conclusions and assume she knows exactly what someone else is thinking. Her thought process is illogical and unsubstantiated, but she's convinced she sees things accurately.

A third form of twisted thinking is what I call the *hero or villain outlook*. When a woman thinks this way, everyone in her life is either a good guy or a bad guy, with no in between. She unconsciously files all her friends, family, and acquaintances as "good" or "bad" in her mental Rolodex.

"You're either for me or against me; here to help me or hurt me."

If she puts you in the villain category, it's a difficult feat to be recast as a good guy.

Other hazardous forms of thinking are directed toward herself. She labels herself with demeaning names. Instead of saying, "I've had a failure," she says, "I am a failure."

She filters out positive comments of praise directed toward her. Her inner voice of criticism quickly counters affirming messages with messages of shame and guilt. Conversely, she can blow one small negative remark out of proportion and remember it for months or years to come. Her damaged filters create and retain negative, rejecting, and hurtful comments, but discount encouraging, positive remarks.

Body Image

One area of significant impact for a woman is how she views her body. She feels deep shame as a result of molestation. She experienced forced exposure and became naked—both emotionally and physically. The side effect for many women is more shame. She has a difficult time accepting her body. She views it as bad and dirty.

A woman also may not be fully aware of her body. One survivor I met said she was so disgusted with herself physically that she had emotionally detached from her body from the waist on down.

"I felt like a big torso walking around with no sexual parts at all."

She couldn't accept the sexual aspect of who she was.

Whether they perceive distortions regarding height, weight, looks, or shape, women who have body image problems can't see reality, even when it's reflecting back at them in the mirror. Instead, they see themselves as if in a trick mirror at an amusement park; the reflection they see—a false image unseen by others—is one of repulsive disfigurement.

Eating disorders become common among survivors. In an attempt to control the distorted image she perceives, she refuses to eat (anorexia) or binges and purges (bulimia) to satisfy her self-hatred.

But not all women are obsessed with being thin.

Those who've endured sexual abuse contribute significantly to the number of overweight and obese people. One theory for this phenomenon is that survivors create their own defense systems by gaining weight. Experts believe this is an unconscious survival skill: *If I'm unattractive, no one will want to get near me.* The protective barrier she builds may be effective in keeping others away, but the walls also keep her from experiencing true intimacy.

Other women may wear layers of clothing to provide false protection. You won't find them scantily clad, which would make them vulnerable. For instance, a woman may wear excessive amounts of clothing to bed to shield her from being touched.

Body distortions cut deeply. The woman you love may profusely reject herself. She's likely to project her disdain for herself on you too, and assume you feel the same way about her. She may accuse you of thinking she's fat and unattractive and believe her body disgusts you.

You can help her by gently assuring her you find her beautiful. The most helpful comments you can make are those that address her nonsexual parts. You may say, "I love your smile," or "You have warm and caring eyes." Her impulse will probably be to deflect your compliments, but they are meaningful and powerful messages to her. Eventually, with your encouragement, she can learn to accept other parts of herself.

Identity

Who am I? What do I really like? What am I good at?

I was frozen for much of my adolescence, stuck in fears and insecurities. Despite my earlier childhood confidence, after puberty I wondered about my worth: *Do I have any abilities to contribute?*

I can remember telling my mom I was convinced I had no special gifts, especially in the light of the obvious talent dripping off my two older sisters. Denise was beautiful and artistic. She could create something fabulous out of nothing. Her bedroom was decorated with incredible style, using a ladder, some scarves, and a plant in a macramé hanging plant holder. As the little sister, I idolized her earthy, creative vibe. She was really cool.

Debbie was also beautiful, with flawless, honey skin. She was an incredible musician. Jazz, blues, and rock, she could play it all. Although her music didn't fit her preppy style—penny loafers and oxford shirts—she had soul. She was an athlete, and, in my mind, the perfect student. Everything she touched succeeded. I admired her. She was my best friend.

Then there was me. I was breathing: that was my gift. I struggled to find myself. I felt awkward and clumsy. I was, and still am, pigeon-toed, and I walked hunched over. My mom would nudge me and say, "Stand up straight, honey."

What I realize now is that I was self-conscious—self-rejecting really—due to my sexual abuse. I looked at my talented sisters and supposed I would be worth more if I could be like them, if I hadn't been abused. I assumed, of course, that they had been spared the violence of molestation. I learned much later I was wrong.

Molestation stole my identity. I didn't know who I was or what I was supposed to do in life. I felt like an intruder—tolerated, not celebrated. Although my mom loved me and built me up, sexual abuse had punctured a hole in my self-esteem. All her comments leaked out of the hole of my broken self-image.

✦   ✦   ✦

Finding our identity after childhood assault is problematic for survivors. In a culture that idolizes beauty and talent, we are inundated with identity messages: "If you're beautiful, you can do anything."

But we don't feel beautiful inside. We find flaws in our appearance, our talents, and most everything else about us. We hide our insecurities about who we are behind the protective shields and masks we created to help survive our childhood. They help us cope in an adult world.

The goal of healing is to live without masks and lay down our shields.

The Shields

Tough Girl

Determined never to be hurt again, she takes on a hard exterior rooted in fear. She's terrified to be vulnerable. When she was trusting and open, she was violated. Now with an inner-vow never to be wounded again, she protects herself with a prickly exterior that broadcasts her message, "Don't hurt me."

Party Girl

She uses her sexuality to anesthetize her pain. Her denial system says, "I'm not hurt by my past." She may feel so unworthy that the lie still propels her to act out. She reasons, *Bad attention is better than no attention.* She's dissociated from her body and her pain. This party girl—perhaps engaging in group sex, one night stands, or prostitution—usually ends her behavior once therapy starts. In other words, acting out is not her true desire. Her sexual freedom is really no freedom at all but a manifestation of poor self-esteem, identity confusion, and anger. She subconsciously may be using others just as she was used. In her mind, it's payback for the wrong done to her.

The Martyr

She's an eternal victim. She controls her environment by acting weak, incapable, sickly, and fragile. She may be the hypochondriac who is plagued with endless symptoms. She wants and needs attention, but she won't admit it. Instead she stages—not always purposely or knowingly—episodes of weakness and breakdown to gain the time and attention of her family and friends. She thrives on crisis. She creates an atmosphere of chaos, yet casts herself in the role of the victim.

The Peacekeeper

She wears a shield of self-sacrifice. She doesn't want anyone to know of her needs—emotionally, sexually, or physically. Her role is to be a fixer. She's a compliant, selfless, non-encumbering woman. I've worn this mask. I still struggle with the thought that I have needs. That means I need someone. It also means I have to let them help me, and I feel unworthy of that help. I struggled for a long time with letting myself become vulnerable.

If she can save the day or be the hero, she's happy. These behaviors take the focus off her perceived flaws and recast her as a wonderful, giving person. She needs to be needed to fill her void of low self-worth.

Self-Esteem

Self-esteem is closely related to our identity and it is another significant area of struggle for the survivor. Self-esteem is defined as the "value and worth of a person as defined by that person." In other words, it's the assessed value we place on ourselves, the "price tag" each of us allots to ourselves. Poor self-esteem is the tragic outcome of sexual abuse and the unseen root beneath many of our problems. Because the wounded person is crippled by a distorted, disfigured esteem, she's ridden with self-criticisms and shaming inner messages. These messages influence her behaviors and decisions. Self-esteem involves feelings, and feelings create behavior.

Wounded self-esteem can manifest in different ways.

The Overachiever

One way broken self-esteem can manifest in the survivor is in her attempt to overachieve. Her gnawing sense of unworthiness and inadequacy motivates her to prove her worth by achievements. Poor self-esteem drives her to perform intensely in an effort to feel accepted and valued. Even when she has found approval in the eyes of others, she pushes herself to accomplish more. She compares herself to others in hopes that she will rise above the rest with her successes.

In the end, the overachiever develops a neatly constructed facade that she hopes will hide her deep insecurities, but she still feels unconvinced of her worth, no matter how well she performs.

The Underachiever

The fear of inadequacy leaves other victims paralyzed by depression and haunted by thoughts of failure. We reject challenges for personal growth and choose the path of least resistance. Our broken self-esteem causes us to settle for jobs far beneath our abilities or choose relationships that are unhealthy and plagued with problems.

Our low opinion of ourselves can perpetuate a life filled with poor choices and devastating mistakes. A deeply rooted message plays in the recesses of the survivor's mind: *You're not worthy of anything good.* We often live according to this subconscious belief.

In his book, *The Search for Significance,* Robert S. McGee identifies four specific false beliefs that many of us hold to, hoping to gain self-esteem:

- I must meet certain standards in order to feel good about myself.
- I must be approved (accepted) by certain others to feel good about myself.
- Those who fail are unworthy of love and must be punished.
- I am what I am. I cannot change. I am hopeless.[1]

When I look at that list, I see my own thinking and still have to make conscious decisions not to fall for the power of seductions.

Sexual Identity

"Am I gay?"

The sweet, gorgeous young girl's eyes pierced mine. She looked to me for an answer as a tear rolled down her cheek. I didn't know her, but her question was familiar.

"Why do you think you're gay?" These were the first words I ever spoke to Sheyenne.

"Because I hate men."

"Have you experimented with other women?"

"No, not yet. But I'm drawn to them."

Many girls wonder about their sexual identity after abuse. Some

---

1. Robert S. McGee, "Introduction. Chapters 3–10," in *The Search for Significance, Seeing Your True Worth Through God's Eyes* (Nashville: W Publishing Group, 1998, 2003), 26.

become promiscuous and have sex with as many men as possible. It's as if a sexual act of their choosing can become the proverbial "shower" and cleanse them from previous sexual trauma. Sometimes the nature of abuse was so painful and humiliating that survivors end up hating men.

Such was the case for Sheyenne. Her abuse was vulgar and degrading. It included penetration with a coat hanger, the stem of a mirror, and other objects inserted into her by her stepfather. He smeared feces on his penis and made her perform oral sex.

When I saw Sheyenne after our first encounter, several months had passed. Her transformation was startling. At first I thought she was a young boy. She approached me with a cigarette hanging out of her mouth and her baseball cap on backward. She was loud and obnoxious.

"Hey Pastor Dawn, it's me, Sheyenne. I go by the name Shane now."

Sheyenne had succumbed to her identity crisis. Her sexual image was shattered. Because of her rage toward men, she had convinced herself she was sexually attracted to women.

From my vantage point, Sheyenne was confused about her sexual identity, but she also found a sense of power from her sexual transformation. The mask she wore was more than the hard, lesbian tough girl. She became a man. I sensed that she positioned herself in the place of power—like her stepfather—to assure herself she would never be abused again.

I told her what I thought.

"Sheyenne, I'm not buying this whole gay persona-thing you've got going on. You're trying to protect yourself."

She looked at me, shocked. And that's what I wanted—to jolt her out of her dissociated fantasy.

"Shhh. I'm not talking about this. But I'll be back, Pastor Dawn."

So far I haven't seen Sheyenne, although I've seen Shane—her alter ego—several times. My prayer is that one day we'll have the chance to talk.

◆   ◆   ◆

Sexual image distortions are rampant among survivors. Becoming sexual beings got us hurt, so we find a sexual image we can live with. Some victims try to shut down their sexuality and become asexual, or, "Just a head walking around." Many women, like Sheyenne, take on a lesbian mask, and some choose to become bisexual. Still others indulge in promiscuous sexual behavior of all kinds.

Sexual abuse distorts the identities of women, and in response, they seek identities that will rebuild their self-esteem while still admitting a sense of insignificance. Their pursuits of meaning and purpose only leave them feeling empty when they have not experienced authentic healing of their wounded selves.

10

GOD AND HER ABUSE

"If God don't make no junk, then what am I doing here?" —Jalynn

By now you've discovered one of the secrets of a survivor: relationships are problematic. A distressing consequence of sexual molestation, the adult survivor is plagued with conflicts in their interpersonal relationships. Without help, both the survivor and his or her partner may have a tumultuous time navigating through relationship waters. The adult survivor also has trouble with the most important relationship of all: her relationship with God.

Trusting God

Forming and maintaining an enjoyable relationship with God Almighty is immensely complicated for a survivor. Their journey with God is often unstable, rife with spiritual mountain-top highs and death-valley lows. That's because trust is an essential building block of any relationship, and trust has been broken. Without it, a strong relationship cannot be established. For her, however, trust is virtually non-existent. It was lost—demolished, really—after her abuse, and now it's difficult for her to relate to (or trust) an invisible God who didn't seem to care or notice when she was being raped and molested. Her trust in both people and in a God who is supposed to "always be there for his children" has been shattered.

Relationships are also built upon the essential building block of intimacy. But even the word *intimacy* is a struggle for survivors. If the woman you love is like many women I've talked to, hearing that God wants to be in an intimate relationship with her is like hearing fingernails on a chalk-board: the phrase sends chills up her spine. The last thing she wants to picture is intimacy with God. The thought is nauseating. Of course, her ability to comprehend true intimacy and closeness with a loving God has been defiled. And since intimacy requires trust, the cycle continues, and her relationship with God often remains troubled.

As I pondered this chapter, I asked female survivors to share their feelings on intimacy and their relationship with God.

Kelly

The abuse did affect my trust. I have a hard time trusting others. When I think about it, I have a hard time turning everything over to God. I try, but I have a hard time not being in control of things. It scares me.

Leslie

Last night, while spending time with God, I silenced everything around me and listened to him. I had an image of God grabbing my ponytail. I know that my God is a gentle God, but with my ex-husband, domination and control were his way of showing me how much he "loved me."

Sara

I don't have the same closeness with God as others do. I force myself to say I love God and wonder why I've never shared my thoughts with anyone, though.

Shar

It's hard for me to know what true love is. It's hard to understand good love, trusting love, safe love. I love God very much, and I know he loves me in a good way. I've asked him to help me with this and he is. God has freed me from the abuse and I have forgiven, but it's always going to be a part of me . . . a trigger of emotions sometimes.

Brindle

I used to feel so condemned, and although I could see God blessing me, I felt unworthy of good and great things for me. But now God has sent me someone who's constantly reassuring me that I'm special and I am worthy of God's best for me. It's like God is using him to be a visual example of his love. So now I am seeing a slow change in myself—like God is still reaching out his hand, and I'm realizing its okay to come before him as I am.

Lori

I feel unworthy. I don't deserve to be in his presence.

Lori's words sum it up for many survivors: "I feel unworthy of God's love." Her gnawing feelings of unworthiness stemmed from an abusive father. Lori's father not only sexually molested her, but he told her God couldn't look upon anything unholy or evil.

"That's you," he told her. "You're impure and sinful."

Lori believed his twisted and convincing lie. I've watched Lori suffer for many years trying to grasp the love and forgiveness of God. She still can't conquer the inner voice that tells her, "God doesn't love the unholy, and that's you."

✦   ✦   ✦

God takes the rap for most of the abuse in the world. I know I had questions. "Where were you, God? If you're such a loving and powerful God, why didn't you do something to stop it?" Some survivors conclude that God didn't love them enough to run divine interference. "I must not be worth saving." "I don't blame you, God, I don't like me either."

Her God-View

How can a survivor understand God as "One who is always present," when it feels to her that he was a "no-show"? God didn't make the rescue. You can understand why the woman you love flounders spiritually.

Her God-image is a convoluted mix of what she believes about him and what she thinks he believes about her. The saddest part is that a distorted God-view keeps her from receiving his love and power to restore, the very things she needs to heal.

Another facet of her healing journey occurs when she becomes aware of her view of God and takes steps to change it.

Her God-image may be . . .

Abusive Father

When a girl is abused by her father or other trusted authority person in her life, the abuse creates great confusion about the character and love of Father God. She equates the twisted attention from earthly authority figures with God's love. She reasons, "If a so-called loving, earthly father can abuse and hurt me in the name of love, then God must be the same way." She's deeply confused about how to love and approach God.

Strict Taskmaster

She may also see God as a strict, intolerable authoritarian who is ready to pounce on her when she does the slightest thing wrong. She ends up living a performance-based life, desperately trying to meet the demands of a stern and task-driven master who can't be pleased.

Ambivalent God

She may say, "God is a distant, far away, uncaring God who is ambivalent and uninvolved. After all, he didn't come when I called." If she carries the belief that God doesn't care about her daily life, she'll try to tough life out on her own. She may dare to call on him if she's desperate, but she wrestles with the fear that he won't come through for her.

Powerless God

An ambivalent God doesn't care to do anything, but this view says, "A powerless God can't do anything." He has no power to stop bad things from happening to defenseless children. She felt abandoned during her abuse and views God as one more person who failed her because of his inability. Trusting a powerless God seems pointless to her.

In spite of believing incredible distortions about God, many survivors still reach for faith as their source of healing. They instinctively know they need a power greater than themselves to overcome their massive soul-wounds.

✦   ✦   ✦

At some point in my healing, I began to see God differently. He did indeed want to stop my abuse, but he had also given men and women free will. He loves us enough to let us make choices. The man who abused me made a horrible, life-altering choice. His choice not only affected him, but it affected me, my husband, and my children in staggering ways.

I also knew that if God stopped every evil act committed against everyone that cried out for deliverance, we would live in a perfect world called heaven. Someday I'll be there, and all my pain will be gone.

Some years later, I did reach out to Jesus for healing and comfort and called on him to restore me. His entrance into my life—not religion, but the authentic presence of the living Savior, Jesus—marked the beginning of my makeover. Body, soul, and spirit, he healed me and continues to heal me. I learned the truth about him: that God doesn't just *have* love, he *is* love. He can't be untrue to his character. He loves each one of us deeply, regardless of what we've done or what's been done to us.

That's who he is.

In fact, we can't earn his love by good deeds or actions. The Bible tells us that while we were yet sinners, Christ died for us. He loved us when we were at our worst—when we were still lost in our sin, God sent his son Jesus to die for us. That is love.

His love and acceptance of us is always extended—even when I felt unclean, unworthy, and filled with shame. God's love covers me. (See 1 John 4:8; Rom. 5:8.)

11

SEXUAL INTIMACY

"I've been the only one initiating sex for months now. If it weren't for me, we'd never have it. Quite frankly, I'm getting tired of being the only one interested in making love. I can't take much more rejection." —Steve

"Why is this my fault? Why am I to blame?"

I was weary of feeling guilt for our broken marriage and even more exhausted from what had become the same pointless argument. Fighting over our sexual life was getting us nowhere—except pushing us further apart.

"Terry, can't you *pleeease* understand? I'm begging you to try."

"I'm trying to understand. But you don't understand me. I have needs, too."

According to my husband, I'd rejected him 49,537 times. From my point of view, I'd pleaded for mutuality in intimacy a million times.

"If you're going to have sex with me, may I please be there?" I was jaded. It seemed to me all he wanted was my body. After countless sexual episodes that had ended in disaster, I was hopeless that things would get better between us.

His pattern of approaching me for sex was predictable: advances came in the middle of the night, while I was in a deep sleep. I explained to him that his nocturnal methods were triggering me.

"When I wake up with you grabbing me, it scares me. I'm not sure where I am or who you are. You're setting yourself up for rejection."

I tried to help him understand, "Sexual abuse survivors don't like surprises. I'd like to be 'present' before we engage in sex."

But to Terry, I seemed unapproachable. Because he feared even more rejection, he decided it was less intimidating to initiate sex while I was asleep.

So he hedged his bets and lost.

It was the fight *that started* the end of our marriage.

◆   ◆   ◆

By now you've probably discovered that your sexual life is a virtual landmine of explosive triggers. That was true for my marriage, and I've found it's true for most couples. On one hand, it might be good news for you to hear that sexual tension is normal and you're not alone. On the other hand, it may dishearten you to learn that your sexual conflict is a serious, pervasive issue and won't just go away. Indeed, the sexual relationship is by far the most sensitive matter you'll face with a survivor, since it involves both of you in the deepest, most intimate and personal way.

Searching for *Normal*

You want a healthy, satisfying sex life. Most men do, and their desire is appropriate. But like many men in intimate relationships with survivors, you may be disappointed to discover her ability to give and receive sex as a beautiful, intimate expression has been stolen from both of you. Instead of feeling pleasure, she often feels confused when she's touched. She doesn't respond to your sexual cues and that hurts. Her sexual encounters aren't marked by ecstasy but instead, with painful, emotional distortions.

Touch triggers her. Unexpected touch is worse. Since she was overpowered and exploited, a woman often resists an approach that's too assertive. She feels vulnerable and afraid to let go of control and freely yield to a sexual encounter. The feeling of being swept away in arousal threatens her.

That doesn't mean you can't ever have an enjoyable sex life together, but you must have realistic expectations. Just when you think your sex life is getting better, she may push you away. She isn't trying to reject you on purpose, but at times she can't cope with the intensely emotional and sometimes terrifying aspects of sex.

Intimacy Derailed

Maybe intimacy wasn't always this way for the two of you. Many survivors have full and free sex lives in the early stages of their marriage before their past issues begin to interfere. Then something happens, and like a light switch, the adult survivor turns off to the idea of sex. If this has happened to the one you love, there are reasons why she's responding this way.

She's Unaware

One possible reason is because she's being triggered in ways she doesn't recognize. In other words, she doesn't realize her sudden disinterest in sex is related to her childhood molestation. She may say, "I don't know what's wrong with me," but unconsciously she's reexperiencing the disgust of abuse and is being traumatized all over again. She's baffled by her repulsion toward sex and feels enough conflict and guilt that she can't perform and would rather avoid sexual encounters altogether. One woman told me, "I had a hard time not acting out during sex. Until I understood what was happening to me, I was so embarrassed by my behavior that I wanted to steer clear of having sex ever again."

If you attempt to engage her for sexual intimacy and she stiffens or becomes inflexible, she's bracing herself to endure what she thinks will be painful to her. It's better to wait and gain her trust than to coerce her.

She's Fighting Painful Memories

Another reason for her coolness toward sex is because her childhood issues have surfaced and she's aware of their connection to her aversion to sex. Once she starts the healing journey, her memories and emotions push their way into the forefront of her thoughts. Sex for her is now an agonizing reminder of her abuse. I tried to explain this common reaction to Steve, a perplexed husband who was upset with his wife's sexual resistance.

"Sex was great before she started dealing with all this abuse junk," he spouted. "Why can't things just be normal?"

"Do you know what normal is for her?" I queried. "Think about it, Steve, sex is associated with the most horrific event of her life. Normal for her is painful. With every touch she experiences from you, her emotions are stirred up. Give her some time. She's feeling too agitated and panicked right now."

For this couple and so many others, a normal sex life has to be cultivated. I know the word *cultivated* doesn't drip with romance and steamy passion, but it can be exciting if you both share the right heart and attitude. Fostering a good sex life has to be intentional, but that doesn't mean it can't also be wonderful.

She Has a Low Sex Drive Due to Abuse

Some survivors have a very low sex drive, if any at all. A reluctance for sex is another defense mechanism to protect her from perceived harm. Her aversion is an involuntary reaction to the sexual encounter, since the act of sex elicits difficult and unwanted emotions. She subconsciously shuts down her sexuality, feeling repulsed and agitated. She's reliving her past.

She Feels Shame for Having Pleasure

Another reason for her disdain could be because during an abuse episode, her body was sexually stimulated and she received physical pleasure. Her body responded the way it was designed to, but she feels doubly betrayed—first by the abuser and then by her own body.

As a result, she experiences shame when she experiences pleasure in sex. She may feel disgusted for needing sex. Her positive sexual experiences trigger her past negative experiences, and she associates pain with the present.

She Has to Numb Out

Many survivors find that in order to have sex, they have to numb out emotionally or even physically. They may use alcohol or drugs as a way to dull their emotions or escape them totally during a sexual encounter. That may be true for your partner. Without going numb, she can't engage in sex.

Listen to Krista's story:

Sexual abuse severely impacted our marriage. I don't even know all the ways it has affected us, but the obvious ones are lack of emotional intimacy and masturbating instead of being together and satisfying each other. Internally, I feel nothing. . . . I have a mental block for all feeling inside my vaginal area. I don't know why or how to unblock it. I can climax externally, but I feel nothing inside, not even pressure. It's like a lumbar block. My response is subconscious—like my body refuses to feel pleasure or pain. Many people who go through trauma experience emotional numbness. But I don't know anyone who experiences physical numbing of the traumatized area. Then again, people don't talk about this subject very often.

She's Triggered

It's possible she could enjoy sex, but things derail her and prevent intimacy. Ask her if you can do something differently. You may be surprised to learn she doesn't like cologne, or she likes it and it adds to her sexual arousal. You may discover the brand of toothpaste you're using, mints, gum, or some other smell is interfering by causing her to have flashbacks. You could be triggering her by the way you touch her or the places you kiss her, or because of the details of the environment— the music or surroundings. One survivor was triggered by her husband's beard. "If he comes to bed with a bristly face and tries to kiss me, I feel nothing but rage." Her trigger may seem nitpicky, but his whiskers were a hideous reminder of the sexual torture she endured from her alcoholic father.

If you're willing to not dismiss her triggers as silly or controlling, you may see better results. Remember, she's a survivor trying to heal, and she wants to feel in control of her body and sexuality. She wants to feel empowered—free to choose what she wants, when she wants it.

Together, once you both gain understanding, you can help her overcome her triggers and enjoy sexual closeness.

The Other Extreme

Some survivors have a sex drive that's on full-throttle at all times. This coping mechanism might be her only way to feel loved and valuable. In this case, she associates her worth and significance with performing sex. When she feels insecure and needs to be reassured of your love, she may press for a sexual encounter.

Other survivors vacillate between a fully engaged sex drive or nothing at all. Her openness to sexual intimacy may change from day to day. This can be particularly confusing for you, her partner.

✦   ✦   ✦

As her partner, it will be difficult not to take her dislike for sex personally, but try to remind yourself her expressions of reserve and frustration are not about you. Her responses are unfortunate effects of abuse, and you're both victims. Often the survivor benefits from hearing the words, "It's not your fault." When it comes to sexual struggles, *you* may need to hear those words: "It's not your fault."

— *12* —

HER INNER CHILD

"I never know who I'm going to encounter. One minute she's smart and sensual, and the next minute she acts like an irresponsible child. I'm not sure if I'm supposed to be her husband or her father." —Gary

Most survivors of sexual abuse feel they've missed their childhood. Forced to grow up too fast, the child who has encountered sexual abuse is abruptly removed from a world of trust and freedom and hurled into a world where she must be alert and on guard. Her carefree innocence is gone, and the vulnerable child is forced into hiding. The happy, playful world she deserves and needs has been stolen, ravaged by the selfish crime of sexual abuse.

Although she's hiding deep within the adult, the inner child is still there. She survived and needs to be validated and loved, and she has a story to tell. For many survivors, this inner child carries traumatic and painful memories. Getting in touch with her often means recovering and or reexperiencing sexual abuse memories.

Delving deep inside to explore the inner child is both difficult and rewarding for the survivor. Most survivors feel that discovering the child within, giving that child a voice, and listening to her cries are important parts of their healing. Many survivors have reclaimed parts of their playful and childlike personalities after being introduced to their inner child and allowing her to release the painful memories she's held.

I'd heard about the inner child—how important it was to find her, listen to her, and integrate her feelings, memories, and pain with mine—but I wasn't interested. I wasn't even sure I believed all that non-sense. But whenever I considered the possibility of my "child within," I felt strong emotions. I despised her.

I thought the little girl in my past was stupid and weak. She should've done something to stop her father. She should have stood up and yelled, "If you touch me one more time, I'm going to scream and tell the world what you've done!"

Instead she retreated. She fled to a hiding place, a safe place, separating herself from the painful experience and burying the memories in the recesses of her soul. I self-rejected for a long time. I'd grown to resent the vulnerable little girl who, I thought, bailed out on me emotionally when she encountered abuse. She was vulnerable, naive, and unsuspecting, trusting others too easily. Her blind trust, however, proved to be detrimental to me, and I was angry with her for it.

Since she ran to the deep places for safety, I felt she might as well stay there. She was of no use to me, so I threw her in the basement of my soul and locked the door. She could only do me harm as an adult. Life was tough and rough, and I couldn't risk having a weak, vulnerable little girl caving in on me.

Still I knew she was there—the inner child—and that she held some of the memories of my abuse. At times I could feel her knocking on the door. I could sense the unrest inside and knew I was silencing her. I wasn't interested in giving her a voice in my life.

Why listen to her? She was weak-willed and powerless. Besides, what good would it do to cry over the situation now?

Then one day we met. I was in church, singing and worshiping God. An intense yet weightless peace fell over the room. Warmth flowed over me. My eyes were shut as I sang that morning, but in the solitude, I saw what seemed to be a movie screen drop down in front of me.

I was having a vision of sorts, an impression I believe was from the Lord. In that vision I saw a little redheaded girl sitting on a playground bench—her toes turned inward as her feet dangled just a few inches off the ground. Soft sobs echoed from her, though she tried unsuccessfully to muffle the cries behind delicate hands clasped over her mouth.

She was alone and appeared to be desperately scared, without anyone to comfort her.

I stood at a distance, my arms crossed. Standing next to me was a figure dressed in white. I knew it was Jesus. Together we quietly observed the troubled redhead. No one spoke a word, but I could see Jesus' eyes filled with compassion as he looked on. Mine were filled with contempt. Then I broke the silence, blurting out in disgust, "Someone should go help that little kid."

"Yes, someone should. I'd like it to be you."

"Why me? She must have done something to deserve this pain. Why should I help?"

Jesus said nothing. He simply looked at me and then gestured with an open hand toward the hunched-over figure of the child. I kicked at the dirt and shifted my weight from one side to the other. I huffed and muttered, "Fine, I'll go talk to the weakling."

The little redhead sat frozen as I slumped down next to her on the bench. Unlike hers, my feet touched the sparse wood-chip covered ground, but my toes were as turned in as hers. I wondered what to do next. As I searched for something brilliant to say, I couldn't help but notice her slender arms and compare them to mine. They were amazingly similar: fair-skinned, and generously spotted with freckles.

Weird. She looks just like me.

"So, what's wrong? What did you do?" I asked.

She shrugged her shoulders, "Don't know."

I was impatient. "Well, why are you crying?"

For the first time, she turned her face toward me and looked me in the eyes. I was astonished. *Dawnie, it's you! I mean it's me. It's us.*

Compassion flooded me and I threw my arms around her. Words of comfort and assurance poured out of me the adult, to me the child.

It's okay. It's not your fault. You did nothing wrong. You're going to be all right.

I soothed and comforted the child—my inner child. I assured her of her innocence. I told her she was forgiven and not to blame. I hugged her again. This time as I embraced her, she melted into me and we became one. Jesus stood nearby. He nodded and smiled. And with that, the vision ended.

With the music in church that morning, I was swept away to another time and another place. Now back in the present, I opened my eyes. Only a few minutes had gone by, but it seemed like hours. The warmth I had experienced earlier was now radiating from inside of me where the little redhead had hugged me around my waist.

I knew God had given me a precious gift, a vision to show me what must take place in my life. If I were going to heal from my sexual abuse, I'd have to do away with the scolding, critical, and fault-finding adult. I'd have to learn to love and accept every part of myself—even the frail and vulnerable child.

Her Child Within

By now you may be wondering if you can handle such a thing as a child within. Or maybe you know exactly what I'm talking about. Like Gary, you may have glimpsed the wounded, hurting child in the one you love. You've seen her face change before your eyes, and instead of conversing with a peer, you're suddenly talking to a six-year-old.

The switch from adult to child can happen quickly, because anything can trigger a woman, causing the inner child to appear. She may feel threatened by something: an angry voice, a touch, a fragrance of perfume or any odor—seemingly random things. Yet for her, those events, objects, or occurrences triggered a feeling, emotion, or memory—or a piece of one—and she suddenly regressed to a younger age.

When this happens, you don't have to fear as though something strange and unusual is happening. Instead, support her by speaking in the same gentle tones that you would use with a child. This soothes her and reassures her that you're a safe person. It also helps to ground her in the present as she works through a painful, perhaps fearful moment.

After I acknowledged my inner child, I learned to nurture her and build trust. Before then, when I was overcome with strong emotions, I suppressed them because I was unable to process what I felt. Throughout my healing journey, I continued to learn more about the broken child inside of me. Instead of dismissing my emotional unrest, I learned to stop and ask myself, "What are you feeling?" Or, "What's wrong?" I often discovered that my circumstances made me feel trapped, afraid, or vulnerable and mimicked the same uncomfortable emotions associated with my sexual abuse.

When I felt anxious, I soothed my fears and reminded myself that I was safe and could exit my circumstances if I wanted to. I assured myself that I was not a helpless child without a voice. I was an adult who could protect and defend myself and get help if I needed to. By engaging in this process, I strengthened my insecure and fearful child and helped her grow and mature.

We All Have a Child Within

The inner child is not unique among sexual abuse survivors. We all have a child within and could benefit from acknowledging that child. We all have suffered pain and traumas, many that could drive a child to split off and retreat to a safer emotional place. The process of finding, listening to, and validating the inner child is valuable to us all.

As your loved one's healing path unfolds, she'll want to come to peace with her inner child—to grieve what was stolen, and to listen to and validate the precious child who survived. Show your love and support as you encourage her along the way.

— *Part 2* —

UNDERSTANDING THE HEALING PROCESS

— 13 —

HEALING STAGES

"It feels like all we do is talk about her sexual abuse. How long do we have to go through this? Some days it seems like she's getting worse instead of better. Why can't she just let go and get on with her life?" —Larry

The woman you love was sexually abused. She can't change her past. Her history is permanently set. Now she has to decide what she'll do with it. In my recovery process, I often said, "Being victimized makes me feel like someone threw mud all over me and then walked away. They've wiped their hands clean of it, but I'm left standing here in filth and ruins."

I was angry that I had to suffer the lifelong results because of the vicious, self-gratifying act of someone else. But that was the sad reality.

The woman you care about has her own decision to make. Will she choose the healing road or remain victimized by sexual abuse? She's a survivor already, but she can be so much more. If she's going to live her life free from the torment of the pain, she'll have to look her abuse square in the eye and make peace with her heartbreaking past. The only way she can be free is to unchain the memories and liberate herself. If she's willing to do that, she can be more than a survivor, she can be an overcomer.

The healing process isn't quick, and it's definitely not easy. Healing from the scars of abuse can take years. I don't want to discourage you, but I want you to understand the reality. Some effects of abuse never disappear. They must be continually confronted and managed as they surface. Other effects can be healed and will disappear.

Unfortunately, some women can't let go of their painful pasts and feel the effects of abuse every day. As Brenda said, "I know I live with unforgiveness and a hard heart, but I can't get past it. I hate him for what he's done to me, and I'll never let it go."

Her healing journey will take time. You will experience moments of excitement for her progress, and those moments will be followed by discouragement when it seems you're re-visiting a mountain you thought you conquered. It may help you to envision her healing process as a spiral, rather than a straight line. She's traveling upward, even though her path seems like familiar territory.

Remember, the journey will be difficult and excruciating, but also rewarding and exhilarating.

◆   ◆   ◆

How will you know when she's getting stronger? Survivors go through stages during the healing process. Most therapists recognize these stages. They are common and relatively sequential, but while some survivors experience every stage in order, many others do not. I experienced several of these stages, but not all. Remember her experience will be just that: uniquely hers. She probably won't move neatly from one stage to another in perfect sequence or timing. But it's important for you to learn the characteristics of each stage so you can help her recognize where she might be in the healing process.

1. Denying the truth
2. Deciding to heal
3. Surviving crisis
4. Remembering
5. Choosing to tell
6. Releasing responsibility
7. Finding the inner child

8. Grieving loss
9. Expressing anger
10. Forgiving
11. Resolving the conflict

Because these stages address the primary areas where survivors struggle in the aftermath of abuse, I've addressed each stage in a separate chapter.

— *14* —

DENYING THE TRUTH

It took me a long time to admit my sexual abuse wounded me. It took me even longer to say the words out loud. But until I did, I wasn't ready to begin the healing process.

If she's ready to admit she was sexually abused—that it was a hideous violation against her and wounded her—she's ready to travel the road to recovery.

This stage is about coming to terms with the fact that she's a survivor of sexual abuse and, as a result, is profoundly injured.

Admitting she's been harmed and still is being harmed by sexual abuse may seem like an obvious step to you, but the vast majority of assault survivors want to minimize their pain or ignore it altogether. I know I did. I wanted to pretend my past had no impact on my present. "It's over and I'm fine," was my attitude.

Most of us bury our suffering for years before we're willing to acknowledge our abusive past and the damage it's done to our lives. Yet the signs are everywhere. Since you're close to her, you undoubtedly see the negative ripple effects of sexual abuse in her life and your relationship. She can unknowingly sabotage her present with destructive behaviors. She's blind to the relationships between her present problems and her past. To you the connections are glaringly evident, but she may protest at the slightest suggestion that her past is the culprit.

Sometimes a survivor is willing to look at her pain only because she's forced to. Physical and emotional troubles can suddenly rush into her life like floodwaters. These symptoms are signals that her emotions can't be held back anymore.

My healing was triggered by an onslaught of panic attacks. I'd never experienced one before. I wasn't even sure what was happening to me. Out of the blue, one morning I woke up startled, overcome with dread and feelings of intense fear. I piled out of bed and frantically paced for over two hours.

I later learned that I was having panic attacks. And they were relentless.

Anxiety bombarded me, fast and furious for five months. The symptoms were unbearable. I sought medical help for relief. But when treatment didn't correct my symptoms, my doctor wanted me to dig deeper. He sent me to a psychologist to investigate the possible underlying issues generating the anxiety.

I was more than reluctant, I was resistant—mad, really.

Why can't this guy just fix me?

Reluctance has a way of succumbing to desperation. So I went, dragging my feet. I'm thankful that my doctor could see what I wasn't willing to acknowledge. My symptoms weren't the problem, but they were telling me I had a deep one, and my issue needed to be addressed.

✦　✦　✦

If she admits to her sexual abuse, she has shown incredible courage. But even after she comes face to face with the realities of sexual trauma, she may question herself and vacillate between "Did it really happen?" and "It wasn't that bad, was it?"

You can help her by not allowing her to deny the abuse or its impact. If she says things like, "It's no big deal," or "It's in the past," support her healing by reminding her that the abuse against her was, indeed, a big deal and significant. This kind of encouragement can keep her from slipping back into denial.

Facing her past and deciding to heal is critical, but you can't push her. She must come to a decision about her healing by herself. She can arrive there faster and easier if she knows you're ready to support her in a safe environment.

— 15 —

DECIDING TO HEAL

Once she admits her sexual abuse happened and that it did indeed scar her, she's faced with a new dilemma: What do I do now? She's acknowledged that the sexual trauma committed against her negatively affected her life, but that won't mark the end of her pain; indeed, the awareness of her abuse is only the beginning of freedom from its affects. She's come to a fork in the road, and she has to make a choice. Will she reach for healing and restoration, or will she pretend that everything is fine now that she's acknowledged her abuse? Some survivors choose to pretend everything is fine until life circumstances become too overwhelming and they experience:

+ Painful depression
+ The breakdown of important relationships
+ A toxic habit growing out of control
+ An inability to cope with everyday life
+ A child leaving home
+ A daughter entering puberty

Engulfing circumstances may be the catalyst for her to recognize, *I can't go on this way. My past is holding me captive.* No matter what it takes to bring her to that point, deciding to heal is a powerful and positive choice.

I like to think of it this way: her decision to heal is a commitment to take a journey. I cannot overstate the magnitude of this choice; the healing journey can be terrifying. It involves surrender and incredible vulnerability. I know I don't like feeling vulnerable. Not many of us do. It's frightening, yet the journey is also invigorating. The survivor begins to believe that healing is possible and therefore worth pursuing, regardless of the perils that may lie ahead. The bottom line is that she moves forward only when she makes the deliberate resolve to claim her wholeness, instead of her current broken condition.

My commitment to heal began when I admitted I was living as a victim of sexual abuse and not a glorious overcomer. Until then, my fear and unwillingness to look at "secrets past" kept me bound under the power and control of abuse. When I finally confessed to myself that I was crippled by the scars of my childhood molestation, I was ready to face the ugly reality of abuse and shed my victim mentality.

Her healing requires a firm and active commitment to face her past. Although she can't simply exert her will and be instantly healed, her determination to grapple with her pain makes healing possible. As she travels the recovery road, she'll have to reaffirm her choice for wholeness and not retreat from the healing process, because recovery is turbulent and disruptive. It involves change—sometimes drastic change. And change often means her discomfort and yours. Unless they make a clear decision for recovery, some survivors find it easy during this stage to throw up the white flag of surrender and quit.

And there may be times when you wish she would quit. Wouldn't it be nice if it could all just go away? But it won't. So your decision to support her during this time is important. She may need you to encourage her to stick with it. Remember, a decision to heal is the threshold for restoration. She's on her way to becoming an overcomer as she walks through this stage.

Healing will come in various forms. Some or all of the following elements are involved in her commitment to heal:

+ Deciding to talk about her abuse
+ Finding a therapist or counselor

- Joining a support group or securing the support of a few close friends
- Trying to remember and to feel and stay connected
- Journaling her progress
- Identifying destructive habits
- Letting go of faulty defense systems

She's taking the first important step down the healing path when she decides to shed her abusive past and pursue wholeness. She probably feels a bit of trepidation at the thought of revisiting painful encounters of sexual assault, but she also has fresh hope. A survivor who is ready to leave her victimization behind is strengthened by her choice to heal.

— 16 —

SURVIVING CRISIS

At some point your partner's past sexual abuse will crash into her present. It's called the Crisis or Emergency Stage. The day of reckoning eventually comes, when the past wants to be known, seen, and resolved.

You'll have no idea when that moment will come. The crisis can be triggered by an event, whether good or bad. It will be a scary time for you both. She will feel (and will be) out of control, and you'll be afraid to see her that way. Survivors fear they're "going crazy." It's important to remember that this stage will pass, but that's exactly what the survivor may not believe: that it will end.

A woman worries that the life she knew has been swept away forever. Your support is exceptionally important in this time. She's the most vulnerable for self-harm during the Crisis Stage.

It was hard for my family to watch me in my Crisis Stage. My past came rushing in without warning and hit like a tidal wave. One night I went to bed feeling normal, and the next day I was sucked out of my life, hurled into a season of depression and panic.

Not everyone experiences a Crisis Stage this radical, but for me it was like a destructive hurricane. My life turned upside down and nothing was familiar. *Normal* was obliterated.

Memories, or pieces of them, begin to surface during this stage. This happens, in part, because she's made the decision to heal and her unconscious mind cooperates by releasing her memories.

When my memories began to push their way into the forefront of my consciousness, they terrified me. I didn't want to remember what happened, to look at the gruesome truth of molestation. At first I thought I was going backward in my healing, but with the assurance and guidance of my counselor, I discovered that having memories was a positive sign. I was starting to feel safe and secure enough in life that I could handle my memories. I wasn't a helpless child any longer, alone and without support. I was strong enough to tackle the past.

The Crisis Stage can also be a stage of disruptions. During this time nothing is exempt from change or impact; everything is up for grabs. You'll both feel the crashing waves of change, and she may be incapacitated by sadness, depression, and grief.

Fred shared his fear for his wife when he watched her deteriorate into depression.

"I'm trying to find out where my wife went. This behavior just isn't her. She's always been the strength of our family. Now all she does is lie on the couch in her pajamas and cry. She hasn't showered, gotten dressed, put on makeup, or been out of the house in days. I'm worried, really worried."

Fred watched his wife enter into the disruptive Crisis Stage. He felt helpless and at a loss as to how to help her. His words describe his helpless feelings: "Her abusive past hijacked our life. And all I can do is sit back and watch it happen."

Other disruptions can happen during this stage. A survivor may experience loss of appetite, sleep, or pleasure in activities she usually enjoys. She'd rather withdraw from social settings and isolate herself.

Her energy is often diverted from the family; her pain can consume her. And it's understandable. It takes an enormous amount of emotional fortitude to face the past. To you it may look like she hasn't accomplished much during the day, but from her perspective, she's drained and exhausted.

In some cases, a husband has had to step in and become both mom and dad for a season. Every case is unique, but in some instances the survivor can't care for her children due to depression or anxiety. We can understand a mother battling cancer or bedridden with a troublesome pregnancy, and we offer support. But the incapacitations that result from sexual abuse bewilder many people. Men often feel too embarrassed to reach out. If this is true of you, please don't struggle alone. Confide in someone and get help and support.

You may also see significant changes in her moods. You won't know what to expect—not just from day to day, but from minute to minute. She can be unpredictable and inconsistent. One husband of a survivor made this comment, "She's driving me crazy. She's up and down so often I can't keep track of her. How can I help her see she's not the only one on this roller-coaster ride?"

You may feel like that, too.

If intimacy hasn't already surfaced as an issue in your relationship, your sexual relationship may become difficult if not impossible at this point. She may want you close, but you may become confused when she says, "Don't touch me." That's because she wants you close for comfort but not for sex. She's developed a complete disinterest in sexual intimacy.

The Crisis Stage is disruptive for her and for you. It's an unsettling, fear-filled, and insecure time. The woman you know is gone, or at least it can feel that way. You may feel more helpless and lost in this stage than in any of the others.

She may be approaching the Crisis Stage if

+ *She cries a lot.* Tears may be frequent, uncontrollable, and unconnected to anything currently happening in her life. She can be highly sensitive.
+ *She's irritable and angry.* You may notice she's often touchy, grouchy, and easily irritated. She becomes impatient and snaps at you for things that didn't seem to bother her before.
+ *She has strong reactions.* It's normal for a survivor who's entering the healing process to react to certain things with hostility. If her abuser was a man, for example, she may make generalities and show her anger and dislike for all men. She may cry at newscasts where the story of an abused child is in the headlines.
+ *She startles easily.* She becomes jumpy and is easily startled.

+ *She withdraws.* She wanders off and begins to isolate herself. Her thoughts are often "someplace else." She has a hard time staying present. Instead of enjoying company, she may become antisocial.
+ *She avoids physical contact.* She wants to avoid hugs, kisses, and physical touch that she once allowed.

These may be indicators that she's starting to connect with her emotions and trauma.

The Crisis Stage is an intense time for both of you. You may feel overwhelmed at the enormity of problems and symptoms that emerge. At times you may be unsure how to help her. You're not alone. Lots of supporters battle with their own frustrations and insecurities throughout the survivor's healing process.

When I'm overwhelmed I remind myself to "take one day at a time." You may need to remind yourself of that, too.

— *17* —

REMEMBERING

Like the Crisis Stage, defined as the disruptive and fearful stage, the Remembering Stage can be defined with two words—agonizingly painful—and can be the longest stage for the survivor.

When memories begin to return, recollections can hurl an adult survivor into crisis. The Remembering Stage goes beyond memories of abuse and includes the process when memories and emotions begin to merge; in other words, she remembers not only what happened but *how she felt* during and after the abuse.

Most survivors go to great lengths to disconnect from emotions. In remembering, we thaw out from our frozen state and emotionally reengage. It's an integral part of the healing process.

My memories bothered me. They were unsettling. But what affected me even more deeply than remembering scenes from the past was the emotional torrent that accompanied them. I was unequipped to handle the intensity, and I panicked. I wanted to run from them, but the words of Jesus brought me strength to remember and feel the past: "Blessed are those who mourn, for they will be comforted" (Matt. 5:4).

In the Remembering Stage the survivor usually suffers many distressing symptoms, many of which seem to occur randomly and linger indefinitely:

+ Sleep disorders
+ Nightmares (her insomnia may be an attempt to escape the torments of reoccurring dreams)

— 112 —

+ Flashbacks—a quick flash of the abuse
+ Heavy clouds of depression
+ Anger, anxiety, and grief

The Remembering Stage is also a time for her to learn how to express her feelings. Because she's been emotionally disconnected, she's not only unsure of what she's feeling, but she's probably also uncertain of how to relay her feelings to you or others. As she learns how to process her emotions and to continue healing, she must also learn how to express and release her emotions in appropriate ways. Your encouragement will help give her strength and courage.

— *18* —

CHOOSING TO TELL

Survivors don't often tell their stories. And when they do talk, it's usually long after the abuse has happened. Only a few people may ever know of the horrors of a survivor's childhood.

I kept my abuse a secret for a long time. Twice I tried to tell someone and get help, but both attempts failed miserably.

My first brave and naive attempt wasn't well thought out. It was a spontaneous act on my part, but I had a surge of courage on one particular day, so I asked the question. I wanted to see if either of my two older sisters held the same secret that I did. If they did, maybe we could help each other. We were getting ready for school and chattering playfully, when I decided to launch into the deep.

"Hey, you guys, does Dad ever do anything . . ."

"Anything what?"

"You know, kind of weird."

"Nope," my sister snapped back and abruptly slammed her bedroom door.

My other sister quietly slipped away. I felt like I'd been doused with a bucket of cold water. I can still feel the chill of rejection that ran through me that day. I knew then that I was on my own.

But I grew tougher. *Deal with this on your own, kid,* I told myself.

I really hadn't planned to tell anyone a second time. My first attempt had flopped miserably, and that was enough for me. Besides, my sisters were my best friends. If I couldn't tell them, I couldn't tell anyone. I didn't trust anyone.

So you can understand my surprise when my mother approached me one day. She looked up from the table where she was sitting and simply asked me.

"Has your father touched you?"

I stood frozen. Finally, I nodded yes.

I don't remember how the following minutes unfolded exactly, but I remember her response as clearly as I can remember anything.

"That snake!"

She pounded the table with her fist and threw her head into her hands. She cried for a long time, but she never moved. My heart broke for her. I wondered how she must be feeling, what thoughts were going through her mind. I didn't think about myself in that moment. I was concerned for her.

In the days that followed, I braced myself for the fallout. I ruminated over what would happen next and who I'd have to talk to. I worried about what I would say.

But nothing ever happened. My confession wasn't brought up again—not for several years.

I didn't recognize it back then as a sixteen-year-old, but I translated my mother's silence into a significant message: "You're not worth making a big deal over." It was unconscious, but the power of that message stayed with me for a long time. It shaped my life. Many years later my mother and I wept bitter tears over what happened. She shared how fear and denial had paralyzed her.

"Oh, how I wish I would have done things differently. I just didn't know what to do."

Her words were enough for me. I've forgiven my mother, for what she knew and for what she didn't know, for what she did and for what she didn't do.

A few years after my mother probed into my sexual abuse, I met Terry. I was eighteen going on twenty-five, and he was a handsome twenty-two-year-old with long brown curly hair. His dazzling smile melted my heart. I decided it was love.

I knew I wanted to tell him about my life, my past, and my childhood sexual abuse, but I was really worried.

What will he think of me?

After our engagement, I told him. Terry and I had one of those long talks common to engaged couples. "I have something to tell you," I said.

"What's that?"

"I was abused when I was a child."

"Oh, really?"

Silence hovered over us.

As casually as you can imagine, I shared the secret that I'd been repeatedly sexually abused as a child. I detached emotionally as I revealed the terrible realities of my past and downplayed its significance. Similar to "How was your day and, oh, by the way, have I ever told I was sexually abused?"

I minimized my abuse when I told him, just as I did after it happened. Terry was probably stunned after I dropped the news on him, but if he was, he didn't show it. Maybe because I presented it in such a blasé way, his response matched mine: blasé. My confession seemed to mean very little to Terry. Later my abuse would be a major factor in ending my marriage.

As I look back on that experience, I realize I was still emotionally disconnected from the impact of my sexual assault. I'd minimized my trauma because I was still under the belief that it was over and done with. And based on the response I received every time I tried to share it—indifference—it was clear to me that there was no real point in bringing it up again. My thought was, *Well, Dawn, you can cry or pull yourself together and overcome your past,* and since I had decided earlier in life that crying was for wimps and babies, I chose the latter. No more crying or feeling sorry for myself. I unconsciously made a note to myself a second time, *Remember, you're not worth making a big deal over.*

I was caught in a dilemma back then. I wanted to tell my story. I needed to know that someone cared about what I'd gone through. I hoped someone would react, make a big deal out of it. I needed someone to react to help me accept what I really believed all along, "This is wrong, tragically and horribly wrong. You don't sexually abuse your own daughter. It's incomprehensible."

I wanted someone to say that to me, to say, "You've been violated in the most devastating of ways. You've been betrayed by the most sacred of all relationships. It's horrific." But no one ever did.

And I couldn't do it for myself.

So I shared my pain with people in a way that protected me from rejection. I couldn't let myself really feel the pain, because when a response didn't meet my sense of injustice, it pained me even more.

So I covered my feelings with indifference. I shoved the hurt so deep inside, I lost touch with how I really felt. I portrayed an image that said, "That's life—it happened but I'm fine."

But I wasn't.

The woman you love isn't fine either.

*   *   *

I'm not sure what you know of her story, but when she starts to heal, telling will become a significant issue. If she decides to tell you, and I hope she will, be prepared. Your support is critical in this moment, perhaps more than any other time. Validate her, believe her, love her, and feel with her. It's okay to cry for her. Hold her. Let her know you're sorry for the pain she's endured.

In the Telling Stage, she may repeat her story over and over again. I admit, it can wear on you and you may feel like saying, "Isn't there something else we can talk about, please?" But please be patient. She needs to talk. Her focus on her sexual abuse won't go on forever, and her preoccupation with her abuse in this stage isn't unhealthy. Learning to share her past experience is an important part of the healing process. At first it may feel awkward and forced for her to tell her story, but the more she tells, the more empowered she will become.

Benefits in Telling

Abuse survivors discover many healing benefits from telling their stories. Of course, results vary, but she can expect to find:

- Support, comfort, and compassion as she tells.
- The deeper intimacy that this kind of honest transparency brings as she shares with her partner.
- Freedom from denial as she tells the truth of what really happened to her.
- Freedom from shame and humiliation as she breaks secrecy.
- New awareness of sexual abuse as she gives others permission to shatter the silence.
- An end to isolation as she finds a community of other survivors to support her.
- Important discoveries about herself.

The light of revelation will turn on as she remembers with more detail the things that have happened to her.

One woman in our support group retold her story often. She shared how her father always gave her a dollar after he sexually abused her. Years later, making love to her husband was incredibly difficult. It carried immense shame. But this night as she relayed her abuse story, she stopped in mid-sentence.

"I just realized something. I was paid for sexual acts. I feel like a prostitute."

Replaying her abuse revealed a lie she had harbored. The shame of being paid for sexual acts was so embedded in her unconscious that she couldn't enjoy intimacy with her husband. She felt dirty and defiled. That's the power of "telling." Talking about her abuse unveiled the debilitating shame and lies that had controlled her and helped her find freedom in the truth.

When Telling Hurts

Be prepared for a wide variety of responses during the Telling Stage, and have realistic expectations. Not everyone is going to be supportive. Some survivors experience negative, hurtful responses when they share their stories. Perhaps she told her family or a close friend for the first time, and the family reacted with anger or denial. The family's response was raw and unrehearsed, but to her it may have sounded as if they were blaming her. People may ask shaming questions such as "Why didn't you stop it?" or questions of disbelief, like, "If what you're saying is true, then why haven't you told us before now?"

These kinds of reactions are painful. I know, it happened to me. But I still believe in the power of telling. Satan works in dark and secret places. Telling breaks the control the enemy exerts through silence and shame and brings freedom to the survivor. It's still painful, however, when she tells her story and she's met with reproach. Since survivors already struggle with shame, it may be difficult for her not to feel as though talking about her abuse back-fired, and she did the wrong thing. She may feel revictimized, want to retreat, and face a temporary setback in her healing.

If this happens to the one you love, be prepared to support her and encourage her. She's taking important steps by sharing her story, and she needs to be affirmed. You can help her by urging her to keep talking. In this early phase of her healing, she will discover that the safest people to tell her story to are you, a support group, or trusted friends and counselors.

— *19* —

RELEASING RESPONSIBILITY

Children usually believe that the sexual abuse committed against them is their fault. In this stage, the adult survivor learns to put the responsibility where it belongs—solely on the abuser. Because we survivors have distorted thinking in many areas of our lives as a result of our childhood trauma, it takes time and intentional effort to redirect our thoughts and beliefs.

We must choose to believe what *is* true, even if it doesn't *feel* true: the abuse was not our fault. Many of us can give mental assent to this fact— abuse is never the fault of the child. But inwardly we believe another story. The responsibility for the harm done to us is often deeply embedded in our minds, and it takes time to drive it out.

Once we have decided the abuse was not our fault and we don't deserve the blame for what happened, we must let go of the excuses we made to minimize the abuser's responsibility. In other words, placing responsibility on the abuser also means we terminate our former justifications on their behalf. I no longer reason away the actions of my abuser. To do so diminishes my ability to acknowledge the depth of my wound. Healing for the survivor includes a firm understanding that the crime committed against her was atrocious and cannot be minimized.

In this stage your loved one comprehends the enormity of the vile transgression against her. Now that she's laid down the responsibility of the abuse and she's not excusing the perpetrator, she'll be able to resolve other facets of her abuse. She'll have to admit that the abuse wasn't an act of love. It was selfish and humiliating. If it applies to her experience, she may have to acknowledge that the people around her—whether they knew of her abuse or not—failed her, and she was left unprotected.

The woman you love will experience even greater emotional relief as she opens her heart to release self-blame and responsibility for her abuse.

20

FINDING THE INNER CHILD

Her innocence was savagely stolen. In this stage the survivor returns to her past and relives, through memories, flashbacks, and sometimes through counseling, facets of her embezzled childhood.

With the reasoning ability of an adult, she can reassess her past but feel the pain through the eyes of her inner child. Because her childhood was stolen, normal adolescent development was critically interrupted. Your survivor lost essential growth during the important developmental stages of her childhood.

As an adult, her perspective is damaged because of her sexual abuse. Natural and crucial maturity was lost as a result. She must go back and reclaim those missing elements.

Physical Development

When a young person develops, her experiences are awkward enough. The child must learn to become comfortable with the physiological changes her body is making and accept her new image. But when an adolescent is abused, the concern and attention she gives to her developing body intensifies. An abused girl may become overly obsessed with changes in her weight, height, breasts, and facial features. She compares herself to others, becomes highly susceptible to teasing or criticism and often suffers with low self-esteem.

During the Inner Child Stage, a survivor must learn to accept her body and reclaim her physical image as beautiful.

Emotional Development

A survivor's emotional development is extremely affected by sexual abuse. Instead of the healthy growth and progress children in non-abusive situations experience, an abused girl must redirect her energy from emotional development to survival. Her focus is diverted to avoiding sexual harm.

It's not uncommon for a woman in the healing process to uncover intense and immature (not fully developed) emotions and act childishly. She is reexperiencing her childish emotions but now understands them as an adult.

Sexual Development

When an adolescent starts to develop sexually, she contextualizes her sexual abuse for the first time. Her emerging sexuality provides a frame of reference for the violation committed against her. She reevaluates what was done to her through the new lens of sexual awareness. This awareness may intensify her struggle with the effects of sexual trauma. A young girl will often become shame-filled and shy or the other extreme, promiscuous and reckless.

Reclaiming her sexuality is a major element of recovery for the survivor. She must reprogram her mind in many areas: her sexual drive and instincts, her body regarding sexuality, and acceptance and enjoyment of the act of sex.

Spiritual Development

As the adolescent develops, her worldview becomes larger. She questions her significance and the role she's to play in life. She filters her questions about God and his existence through her experience of sexual abuse; she wonders why bad things happen to innocent people.

Part of a survivor's healing is to discover she is more than a sexual object. Her past abuse does not disqualify her from God's love or his plan for her life. When the inner child grasps God's love—that she is beautifully made and accepted by him— she can bloom into the woman God created her to be.

Cognitive Development

As her cognitive thinking develops, a child's ability to comprehend the abuse that transpired against her increases. A survivor often reexperiences and therefore, reinterprets her sexual assault. In the Inner Child Stage, she may retrace certain aspects of childhood in hopes of recapturing the things she missed. It's not uncommon to see an adult survivor becoming more playful or finding interest in games, activities, and entertainment that are usually aimed at an adolescent. You may also notice that she cries easily and seems ultra-sensitive. Again, her emotions are being felt and expressed as a child.

Social Development

The child victim is deprived of normal social development once sexual abuse occurs. Cultivating friendships can incite fear and anxiety. A survivor is often confused about proper boundaries in relationships and can become possessive of friends or find herself on the other end of the spectrum as a loner. Relationships with the opposite sex are problematic and awkward; she's unsure of appropriate behavior and can easily participate in sexual misconduct. In healing, the adult survivor recognizes her social skills are often immature and childish, and her relationships are plagued with rejection, jealousy, and insecurity.

As the survivor heals, the child within heals, too. Once the woman you love possesses greater emotional and spiritual wholeness, you'll notice a new maturity emerge. She's finding her way through childhood hurts, and in so doing, she's finding peace.

21

GRIEVING LOSS

Most survivors haven't taken the time to name the many losses they've experienced, let alone grieve them. In this stage, the overcoming adult becomes aware of her losses and begins to grieve them. By allowing herself to mourn what was taken from her, she honors her pain and finds the strength to release it.

When I finally looked upon myself with compassion, when I embraced my pain and acknowledged my right to be wounded, my tears began to flow. I cried almost every day for weeks. I realize now I was in the Grieving Loss Stage, mourning the loss of my childhood and grieving for the precious little girl who was decimated.

Think about the woman in your life who was assaulted. She's sustained many significant losses. At times she may weep and feel profound sadness. Don't be alarmed. Her grief is normal in this stage of healing, and it's different from depression.

Unlike depression, which is a sense of hopelessness and bleak futility, grieving serves an important purpose. If she doesn't get stuck in grief, her mourning will lead her through the passage of pain into the freedom on the other side. One of my favorite Bible verses was especially meaningful to me during this time: "Weeping may remain for a night, but rejoicing comes in the morning" (Ps. 30:5). I like to say it this way: *Joy comes through the mourning.*

She's suffered many losses and needs time to honor them.

Loss of Childhood

We were children, unsuspecting and trusting. We wanted to laugh and play like other kids, but something happened to interrupt our carefree life. Something awful and bad. Now we stand covered in shame and stare at others through hollow eyes, wondering if anyone knows, if anyone can tell. Our cheery, uncomplicated childhood was stolen. We were frightened, anxious, and insecure most of our days. We survived by becoming calculating and vigilant.

I recall a session in our support group when we were discussing our childhood memories. One woman spoke with sarcasm, "Childhood? What childhood? All I can remember from mine is the wooden floor in my bedroom. I spent most of my time hiding under my bed trying to escape from my stepfather. If that's what you mean by childhood—staring at the grain in the wooden slats—then I had a long one."

Loss of Nurture

Every child deserves to be loved and cherished. They need to know that they are wanted and cared for. Acceptance and nurture provide the foundation on which children build their sense of safety and security. And doesn't every child deserve to be safeguarded from the atrocities of the world?

As children, we look to our parents or other close trusted adults to protect us, shelter us, and meet our emotional needs. In the economy of children, nurture plus protection equals love. This equation doesn't exist for abused children. Instead of being cherished, they feel abandoned, neglected, and unloved. Tragically, abused children learn that the world is not a safe place. They discover they're unprotected.

We cannot always blame parents for their children's abuse. Many parents were unaware of the harm done to their children. But something was still stolen that can never be replaced. Abused children live their childhood alone—with a secret, and that secret separates them from the love and nurture of others in their families.

In circumstances like mine—where the abuse came directly from a parent—the loss of nurture is unfathomable. I felt alone. Alone in this sense: if anyone was going to take care of me, it was going to be me. No one took interest in my needs, nor could they. They had no idea what my needs were. I wasn't about to burden my mother by being needy. I learned to become self-sufficient and strong.

The woman you love was deprived of nurture in childhood. This means that in adulthood, she can swing between two poles in her response to her lack of care. One response is that she can be dependent and needy, and often feel like her emotional needs are unmet. And when a survivor feels neglected, take cover. She can rage with hostility, demanding more attention. When she realizes her angry tantrum is not an effective way to find affection, she can become passive and dejected. She can sulk and accuse you of rejecting her. This co-dependent behavior—a condition where she becomes addicted to you to find love and acceptance—can create additional havoc in your relationship.

Although you may be giving her all you have—being sensitive to her needs and wants—she may still complain that it's not enough. You can become perplexed about how to show her that you're trying your best. The problem is she has a black hole in her emotional container. Because she was robbed of nurture in childhood, her struggle is internal. The emptiness she feels can't be fixed by you, no matter how much love and attention you try to offer her.

My point is illustrated by the following words I received in a letter from one survivor.

"I know my angry actions are destructive to my marriage, but I can't express to you the void I feel inside. Why isn't his love ever enough? I want more—I need more."

A second response demonstrates the detached "tough girl." She is overly self-sufficient; you won't see her weak or needy. She won't allow it.

I fell into this category.

My dad was a Marine for four years, just long enough to shape him for life. His service shaped my life, too, because his military background made him tough and commanding. My two sisters and I learned to "buck up" and get things done. Over time, all of us girls developed our response to his parental style and abuse.

My oldest sister, Denise, rebelled and pushed back. I saw that this response was too painful for my mom, and I didn't want to go that route, although I admired my sister for just doing her own thing. She still doesn't acquiesce to what others say or think about her.

My middle sister, Debbie, cried a lot. She was sensitive and emotional. Her tears flowed easily, but that wasn't for me either. I couldn't give my dad the satisfaction of seeing me cry. So I landed somewhere in between my two sisters. I stayed out of trouble as best I could, but I became detached. I boarded up the windows to my soul and guarded my heart. I looked strong and self-sufficient, but I was emotionally removed.

When I met my husband Terry, he liked my independence—at first, until we realized I had a hard time receiving love. I denied that I wanted it or needed it. My hard exterior loudly broadcasted, "Don't get too close to me." He often called me a porcupine, declaring I was prickly and unaffectionate. He was right.

Other survivors feel the same way. Depriving a child of nurture conditions them to protect and nurture themselves. They often build impenetrable fortresses—walls intended to protect but that, in truth, close them off from accepting love and care.

Loss of Memory

I love watching my children—now all adults and married—come together for family events. They laugh hysterically as they reflect back on their childhood memories. It thrills my heart to watch and listen to them and to know that, because of God's grace, they feel as though they had a great childhood.

They have a priceless gift: their memories.

Our memories, both good and bad, help to remind us who we are and where we've come from. Our history is part of our identity.

But for survivors, whole pieces of childhood experiences are missing, memories are completely forgotten. The pain and trauma of abuse was too much for the tender psyche of the child and she's blocked it out. But repression, psychological amnesia, can wipe out pleasant memories too.

This absence of memory is another significant loss for the person overcoming her abusive past. Many adult survivors flounder in an attempt to "find themselves." Because important pieces of their childhood are missing, many feel a loss of identity and unique purpose. They feel they've been ripped off yet again.

Loss of Control

I always wondered why I had a strong, angry reaction to situations where I was given "no choice." It was important for me to have a voice in the decision-making process. I've discovered that the need for control is a common response to sexual abuse.

As children we were overpowered; our right and ability "to choose" was stripped from us. Silently, we surrendered to the humiliation of sexual assault. While inside we were screaming, outwardly we were dismissed. We learned our voice was meaningless.

As adult women, many abuse survivors battle with feelings of insignificance. They wonder if their desires or wishes matter to anyone. In an attempt to validate themselves, many women overexert their wills, determined not to be silenced again. We can understand why survivors might err on the side of belligerence.

On the other end of the spectrum are women who are excessively passive and dependent. Even though they grew up to be intelligent, inside they may still feel small, inadequate, and insignificant.

I talked to one woman who was in her recovery process. I took special note of her because she seemed bright and witty, and I enjoyed her personality. That's why it surprised me when she shared, "I'm paralyzed when I need to make decisions. I don't trust myself to make the right one. If anything, I have an uncanny ability to choose the wrong thing." Because she was forced to forfeit control over her body, her most sacred possession—she questioned her ability to discern right from wrong. "I'm always confused. I'd like to trust my own instincts, but I'm afraid my instincts are bad."

Her helplessness communicates to others, "I'm incapable of taking care of myself. I need you to survive." Although it may seem ironic, passive dependence is her way of gaining control. It says, "I am released from the responsibility of life and rely on you to make the decisions for me." Her response forces others to make wise decisions for her and absolves her of liability.

Loss of Self-Esteem

Survivors also suffer the loss of healthy, positive self-esteem. While we were children, we assessed our value based on the love and nurture we received. When someone more powerful than us—an authority figure—assaulted us, we assumed it was our fault. After all, we're required to respect adults; they're always right and know "what's best for us." The obvious conclusion for a naive and trusting child is, "I must be bad."

When children evaluate themselves and decide they are bad and naughty, they've already begun to suffer from lifelong consequences of damaged and often irreparable self-esteem. Too often degrading sexual assault steals yet another piece of our lives: our ability to feel loved, accepted, and valued.

Loss of Trust

Sexual abuse is a tragic violation of trust and one of the saddest results of the child's ordeal. She feels betrayed in the most personal and intimate way. With no assurance of anyone's true motives, the child feels utterly abandoned. She carries her secret alone.

But living a life with no one to trust is painful. It's also not practical for a child whose very existence depends on adults. To survive, the child may fantasize about the goodness of a person and recast them as her hero, instead of admitting they have harmed her. As a result, the child blurs realities, confuses loyalties, and mistrusts others.

Another disheartening distortion of trust is found in victims' inability to trust themselves. We lose faith in ourselves; our self-confidence is destroyed. We frequently wonder if our perceptions and judgments are sound. "Are my feelings accurate, or is my thinking twisted?"

This inability to trust ourselves and others follows us into our adult lives. It troubles and threatens our relationships. Because trust is the foundation for all intimacy, impaired trust obstructs the closeness we desire with one another and were designed to achieve.

My trust was eroded in childhood and continued to crumble in my adult life, especially in my marriage. My words weren't meant to be threatening, but my husband felt uncomfortable when I told him I needed him to help me trust. He felt frustrated that I couldn't have blind confidence in him when his behaviors felt destructive and damaging. When he hid things from me he said, "I'm trying to protect you," but I didn't feel protected. I felt deceived. Trust—or more accurately, the lack of trust—was a toxic wedge between us. For me, trust equaled respect. When I couldn't trust Terry, I acted in ways that were disrespectful to him.

You can build trust with your survivor. But gaining her confidence will take time. It also will take intentionality. Because earning her trust is a fragile pursuit, you can lose ground quickly by making the wrong move and have to begin the work of healing all over again.

Fostering trust with a survivor is a complicated and delicate issue. Keep in mind, however, that most survivors want to learn how to trust. We want to find a trustworthy person to open up to.

If you want to build trust:

+ *Be trustworthy in the little things.* Expect to be tested on this one. She's watching you to help her decide if you can be trusted. Be reliable. If you can't be on time or remember to do an errand for her, how can she trust you in the big things?
+ *Keep your word.* If you make a promise, see it through. Realize that in giving your word, she may believe you've committed to more than you think you have. Her expectations may be set too high for anyone to achieve, so be clear. Don't allow her to assume you're going to do something if you know you have no intention of following through. You might feel you're keeping peace or protecting her by ignoring conflicting expectations, but pretending you're going to keep a commitment will explode in the end.

- *Be honest.* Tell the truth, no matter how difficult it is. Don't hide things from her, even if you think she's too fragile to hear it. Respect her and give her the right to handle information, regardless of its nature. I'm not suggesting that you be insensitive—truth without love is cruel. But I also believe that love without truth is cruel, too. Your honesty will build trust in a big way. Share your shortcomings. Tell her what you like and don't like; give her honest feedback when it's appropriate. She may not like what you're telling her. She may rage and spit and sputter, but in the end, she will respect you for your integrity. And that means more trust.

- *Don't abuse your power.* Remember her perpetrator was probably someone in a position of trust. When it comes to authority figures and authority itself, she's resistant. This is the area where her trust was broken to begin with, so it's logical that she's confused about power and authority. If you're overbearing or hotheaded, you'll probably find her attacking you back. If she does yield to your heavy authoritarian style, don't be deluded into thinking you have her trust. It usually means she's afraid and trust is a long way off. Be sensitive on this point.

Loss of Sexual Enjoyment

Sexual intimacy for the survivor is greatly distorted as a result of sexual abuse. How can the survivor ever see the act of sex in the way God intended, as pure and beautiful? That lens has been shattered, and the survivor's perspective is damaged.

Many survivors are riddled with excruciating memories, flashbacks, fears, and anger during sexual encounters. These triggers were awful for me.

I longed to enjoy intimate moments with my husband, but I felt like there were more than two of us in the bed—my abuser was there, too. Before I could receive Terry's loving and caring touches, I had to fight off the flashbacks of abuse.

I have to admit, my struggle with painful memories in those moments didn't lead up to great romance. Terry felt rejected numerous times by my responses to his attempts to love me. I couldn't quiet the noise of the past long enough to enter into the beauty of the present moment. Most of our nights of intimacy ended in vicious arguments.

The loss of sexual freedom in romance is one more way survivors have been robbed. Sexual intimacy is supposed to be one of the most precious gifts a husband and wife can share. But for the couple with abuse in one or both of their pasts, making love often feels like anything but love.

One man I talked to named Jerry described his heartbreak over the lack of sexual intimacy with his wife Sandy. She was having problems expressing herself sexually, stating that she "felt dirty." When Jerry started to make sexual advancements toward her, she shrugged him off, rolled over, and pretended to be asleep.

"I hate her father," Jerry spat out as he slammed his fist into his other hand. "His selfish acts of lust didn't just steal from my wife sexually. He stole from me too. He's ruined both our lives."

Sandy hurt, too. She wanted to be a wife who could share intimacy with her husband. But she continuously avoided sex with Jerry. On nights when she could no longer refuse him, she fought to stay present.

"I feel like I'm having an out-of-body experience, as if it's happening to someone else. I'm at the top of the room looking down on it all."

Sandy was dissociating—severing her emotions from her actions—while having sex. Dissociation is one of many symptoms of sexual dysfunction. Women in the process of recovery often experience others:

+ Difficulty being aroused and feeling enjoyable sensations
+ Negative feelings such as guilt, shame, fear, anger, outrage, or disgust when being touched
+ Disturbing sexual thoughts and images
+ Hatred toward sex or feeling like sex is an obligation
+ Inappropriate sexual behaviors or sexual compulsivity
+ Inability to achieve orgasm
+ Detachment or emotional distance while having sex
+ Fear of sex or avoiding having sex

The survivor reclaims her dignity when she grieves the losses of her stolen childhood. The tears she sheds are cleansing to her soul. She may pass through the Grieving Loss Stage several times. You honor her by mourning with her. You help her by extending hope and assuring her she's stronger for facing her loss.

22

EXPRESSING ANGER

I love the movie *Forrest Gump*. In one poignant scene, Forrest and his lifelong friend, Jenny, walk down a dusty road together—the road that leads to Jenny's family home, the place where she was raised, and the place where she was sexually abused.

When Jenny sees her childhood home, she erupts with rage. She grabs rocks and hurls them at the old, dilapidated house. When she can't find any more rocks, she reaches down and peels off her shoes and heaves them at the house, too. Then she slumps to the ground, broken and sobbing. Forrest narrates as the scene closes and says, "Sometimes there just aren't enough rocks."

The Anger Stage is about getting in touch with intense anger. Like Jenny, abuse survivors have to be willing to "throw the rocks" and release the rage within them. But also like Jenny, they have to direct their anger in the right direction, toward the abuse, the abusers, and the people who didn't protect them.

Until the healing begins, survivors are angry—very angry—but at the wrong people and for many of the wrong reasons. Once the healing process begins, they learn how to direct anger in ways that are beneficial and therapeutic. Many therapists have said, "Anger is the backbone of healing." Abuse survivors are empowered when they feel their anger and release it in constructive ways.

If the survivor you love is feeling more intense anger than what you're accustomed to seeing, it may be a good sign. Her anger can mean she's done stuffing her pain and she's ready to tackle the rest of the healing process.

That doesn't mean this isn't a challenging time for you. When the survivor begins to access her anger, she can become intense and hostile. Her memories are rushing to the surface and oftentimes challenging emotions with them. It may be hard for her to differentiate between the past and the present.

This process is called *transference*. She's really angry about how her uncle offered to put her to bed at night and then fondled her breasts. But she's directing her anger toward you for being five minutes late. Your "infraction" unconsciously gives her an opportunity to tap into all the other times people have hurt her. Her reaction seems over-the-top to you, and no wonder; her words are meant for her abuser.

Anger transference is common to all survivors. I know I misdirected my anger at others, namely Terry. I didn't know I was doing that, and for a long time I didn't know why the rage inside me was so powerful. I falsely assumed it was because the other person deserved it, because they did something to upset me. Later, I realized I was jam-packed with rage.

Because she feels safe with you, she may fire at you as an easy target in an unconscious attempt to rid herself of some of the anger she feels. But if she's in the healing process and working with a counselor, she will learn constructive and positive ways to purge the anger she's carried for years.

Her anger is real, understandable, even justified. But left unharnessed it's destructive. In releasing her anger properly by "throwing the rocks," she finds relief and simultaneously, gains more control.

For more on anger, see chapter 4, "Emotions and the Beginning of Healing."

— *23* —

FORGIVING

All the stages of healing are important, but forgiving has the greatest power to bring deep release and lasting restoration.

Once she's ready to forgive, she's free. She's no longer a victim chained to the past. She can live and flourish triumphantly in the present. I like to think of it this way, "In forgiveness she becomes more than a survivor, she's a thriver."

But forgiveness is not given for the benefit of the abuser; she forgives for herself.

When she's ready to cast off the oppressive burden she's carried for so long, the sexual assault loses its power to control and manipulate her life. Without true forgiveness, she'll remain stuck in her pain. All the other work she's done in her healing process becomes futile.

Forgiveness is a powerful force, yet every survivor will forgive at a different pace. The woman in your life will forgive when she's ready. She can't be forced. Because we understand the importance of forgiveness, we want to see it happen as soon as possible. But be careful not to press the assault victim to let go of her hurt. If she's not ready to release her pain, pressing her will backfire and possibly delay her healing.

I made the mistake of forgiving too readily, before I looked at the depth of my abuse. I was told by well-meaning leaders that if I wanted Jesus to forgive me, I had to forgive my dad. I wanted to be free from the past, so I quickly forgave.

I thought I'd found the magic bullet to fast healing—the short "checkout line" only a few knew about. I was finally done with this whole sexual abuse thing. After all, "I've forgiven my dad."

Over the next year or so, plaguing thoughts of sexual abuse continued to trouble me. But since I'd forgiven, I thought I should ignore them. So I dismissed the thoughts and tried to go on with my life—unsuccessfully.

I misunderstood forgiveness. Easy forgiveness wasn't an instant remedy or quick fix for my abusive past. I soon found out that there are no shortcuts on the sexual healing journey. Indeed, there can't be.

What Forgiveness Is Not

True forgiveness doesn't mean she'll forget. If at long last she's recovered her buried memories, then she's received more healing. How then, can forgiveness—another healing element—bring her back to amnesia? Deep hurts can't be erased or wiped out as if they've never happened. The power of forgiveness is in remembering. In the face of the hard facts, forgiveness says, "I choose to let go, to relinquish my right to hurt you for hurting me." However, what many survivors do forget in time is the sting of pain associated with their abuse.

Forgiveness also doesn't mean she's finished healing. Some survivors falsely assume that real forgiveness must mean they can no longer sort out the feelings and issues related to their abuse, and therefore they thwart complete healing. "I've forgiven so it's all over now," they say. I wish it were that simple, but I don't think it is. Forgiving is a necessary part of the healing process, but the woman in your life has to have permission to revisit the pain, talk through her abuse, and process the residual effects as long as she needs to.

Forgiveness also doesn't mean she has to be reconciled to the abuser. In some cases, to resume a relationship with the one who hurt her would invite more abuse. In other cases where reconciliation is possible and desirable, forgiveness paves the way. But reconciliation is not required for her forgiveness to take place. An injured party can forgive an offender without the offender ever knowing—whether they are deceased or alive.

Forgiveness also doesn't excuse bad behavior. What happened to her is inexcusable, and it's never going to be okay. The offense is not dismissed by the act of forgiving. Forgiveness involves taking the abuse seriously. Releasing someone from their sin against her isn't an attempt to pass off the assault as inconsequential or insignificant.

Additionally, when the one who's been hurt finally forgives, the abuser is not absolved from all consequences. It will mean, however, that she doesn't harbor a desire for revenge or wish that something bad will happen to the one who wounded her.

Lastly, forgiveness isn't a quick fix. But that doesn't mean it's not miraculous. Forgiveness is divine and powerful and when combined with other important elements of healing, forgiving brings emotional, physical, and spiritual recovery.

And the wonderful thing is that, no matter her circumstances, the woman you love possesses the power to forgive. Some people believe we have to be asked by the offender before we can forgive. But this isn't true.

Remember the words and actions of Jesus. While his wounds were still fresh and he was bleeding and dying on the cross, he whispered, "Father, forgive them, for they do not know what they are doing" (Luke 23:34). Jesus released forgiveness to those who brutally hurt him. His words indicate that those he forgave didn't understand the immensity of their actions or their eternal impact. It's also clear they didn't ask to be forgiven. This means she can forgive without needing to hear her abuser ask for forgiveness.

Forgiving Herself, Forgiving God

The two beings we most often forget to forgive are God and ourselves. But the truth is, we don't actually forget. We're typically unaware that we harbor resentment toward ourselves and God. We don't want to admit we're resentful. Yet many of us are angry with ourselves and God.

Very angry.

It may sound sacrilegious to think we must forgive God. But forgiving God doesn't mean he did something wrong. Of course he didn't.

Survivors have an expectation of how a "loving God" should have responded to our abuse. When our expectations—and we all have them whether we realize them or not—weren't met, we became angry, hurt, and bitter. We often distance ourselves from God or conclude that he is neither fair nor trustworthy.

The woman you care about most likely has her share of unending, agonizing questions:

"Where was God when I was molested?" "Why didn't he stop it?"

She wonders why God would allow abuse at all.

No pat, universal answer can soothe every wounded heart, although counselors and pastors alike have tried. She'll search for a comforting answer to that perplexing question until she finds peace. Forgiving God is part of answering, "Where were you when I was being abused?"

As I sought to understand God's attitude and response to my abuse, I found comfort in believing God was there with me, feeling my sorrow, grieving my pain, just as he was with his own Son during his death on the cross.

I also understood that if God stopped every single person from committing horrific acts of violence against the innocent, we would live in a perfect, flawless world. Why then, would we need a Savior? Jesus would have died in vain.

But God is love. He doesn't just *have* love, he *is* love. His love includes giving us a free will. Sadly, many use their freedom to hurt others.

Our other difficulty in forgiveness is giving *ourselves* grace. I easily forgave my father, but I was hard as steel on myself. I gave myself no mercy or compassion. Eventually I realized my lack of self-compassion was unforgiveness. I wasn't letting myself be freed from my own judgments about me.

A child who is abused has committed no wrong, and she's never to blame. Logically, your loved one understands that, but deep inside, she's captive to her own self-judgments. She's not consciously aware of it, but she's holding herself responsible for her sexual assault. She did nothing wrong, but she feels culpable.

Why didn't I stop it?

I should have told someone. Maybe then it would have stopped.
That's what I get for being a stupid, gullible kid.
It's my fault for being at the wrong place at the wrong time.
Maybe I asked for it. After all, the attention felt good.

Her list of lies is endless, and she can stay angry at herself for a long time. She needs to release herself from blame and unrealistic expectations and remind herself, a child is never to blame for her abuse. Forgiveness of herself is another important step toward recovery.

Before She's Ready to Forgive

A few essentials need to be in place so she can forgive and release the past:

1. She's made the decision to heal.

This means she's determined not to be a victim of abuse. She's prepared herself to adopt a new mind-set: she wants to be free from the haunting and reoccurring thoughts of her abuse, free from the control of those emotions and memories. Instead of rehearsing her pain when memories arise, she's ready to replace wrong thoughts with truth and claim victory.

2. She can talk about her abuse.

She's freed herself from the dark secret that controlled her, and she can talk about it, at least to one other person. That doesn't mean the process has become easy, but it does mean she's not in denial about what happened, and she knows talking to the right people will bring her more healing.

3. She understands who's responsible.

She knows she's not accountable for the sexual abuse done to her, and she places blame where it belongs: squarely on the shoulders of the perpetrator. She doesn't justify the corrupt actions of an abuser, but she's able to feel compassion for the soul of the one who hurt her. This process doesn't always happen right away; compassion may follow in the days, months, or years ahead, but forgiveness makes it possible.

Steps to Forgiveness

The hard part of forgiveness is for her to arrive at the place where she's ready to let go of the offense committed against her. Once she's there, however, the act of forgiveness itself is an act of her will and is accomplished when she takes these steps:

1. She asks God to help her take this act of obedience.
2. She admits she can't forgive on her own and relies on God's divine strength.
3. She tells God from her heart what she needs to forgive. She may even have a list prepared and can read it to God.
4. She acknowledges her sinful response to the offense and receives God's forgiveness for herself.
5. She releases the offense to God and visualizes placing her pain at the foot of the cross of Jesus Christ.

Once she's freed from the painful chains that bound her, she can move on with her life without the burden of bitterness; she refuses to look back in anger.

Some survivors have found it helpful to forgive once they write a letter to the person who harmed them. I have heard it called the "poison pen letter." The letter is not written to be sent, rather it is written as a way for the survivor to remember and release the offense. Some people create a ceremony and destroy their lists and letters, symbolizing the end of the link between themselves and their offenders. Other survivors visualize placing their list on a raft and watch it drift gently away down the river. Still others burn their letters and scatter the ashes. By using a tangible expression of forgiveness and release similar to these, the woman you love can find release and separation from her wounds.

The Benefits of Forgiveness

Most of us are already convinced of the power and purpose of forgiveness in healing. But some survivors still protest, "Why on earth should I forgive?"

Many ask the question, and if that's true of the woman in your life, she's not entirely persuaded of this one truth: forgiveness is for her benefit, not for the perpetrator's.

Forgiveness benefits her in many ways:

+ Forgiveness leads to inner peace. She can be free from the torment of her past.
+ Forgiveness removes roadblocks in relationships and with God. Her compassion and empathy for others is restored through forgiveness. Forgiveness allows her to love more fully.
+ Forgiveness helps decrease her anger. It lessens the likelihood that her anger will be misdirected toward the innocent.
+ Forgiveness frees her from the sadness and depression that come from bitterness.
+ Forgiveness releases her from the power that both the offense and the offender hold over her. She's in charge of her attitude and outlook. She's no longer enslaved by the actions of another.

Forgiveness gives us closure from the past because we invest our emotional energy positively. Instead of remembering and revisiting the horrors of the past, we focus on a bright and joyful future.

The beauty of forgiveness sets a prisoner free—me.

— *24* —

RESOLVING THE CONFLICT

She's moving forward, making substantial strides toward a new future. That's the goal of healing.

In the Resolution Stage, she's no longer stuck in the pain of the past, but she now faces her future with anticipation. A fresh wind of hope blows through her soul. She begins to rebuild her life and dream again. Aspirations for a fulfilling life were stolen, but she's freed to discover her gifts, talents, and callings that had gone untapped.

The Resolution Stage is a time of adventure as she finds the courage to explore her identity. She's ready and willing to try new things, no longer stalled by the rejection that once paralyzed her. A new person begins to emerge. You'll see glimpses of her restored personality. Her true self was shattered in childhood, but now, with healing, she begins to find herself.

This stage is also a time of integration. The child within and the adult woman merge to create a beautiful and unique individual as she finds God's intentional design for her. She may revisit other aspects of the healing stages, but in the Resolution Stage, she's more determined to come through to the other side.

Setting Aside Her Defense Mechanisms

In resolution, she understands she's not responsible for her abuse. But she's also willing to recognize that some of her responses to abuse— while understandable—have been detrimental to herself and to others.

During this stage she learns that resorting to her previous skills for coping is old, victim-focused living.

As she learns, she'll make purposeful attempts to put down her defense weapons. (It won't be easy; she's relied on them for a long time.) Some of those weapons included:

+ *Repression and suppression.* She's used these techniques to survive the pain of trauma, but in healing she refuses to rely on memory-blocking methods to cope. She chooses to embrace her memories and work through them.

+ *Blaming and projecting.* In the past she blamed herself for everything, or chose an opposite response, refusing to accept blame for anything because her broken self-esteem couldn't absorb the guilt or responsibility. She may have used projection—casting her undesirable feelings, motives, or thoughts onto others in order to avoid being responsible. But in this stage, she becomes accountable for her own feelings.

+ *Masking and shielding.* She used to hide her true self behind false personas, such as the tough-girl image, the overachiever, the happy party girl, etc. But as healing progresses, she learns to allow her real essence to unfold and refuses to pretend to be someone she's not.

+ *Victim identity.* She moves past self-pity and the "everybody's out to get me" mind-set. No longer a victim, she's finally come to a place where she's in charge of her destiny.

Confronting Her Abuser

During this stage she may want to confront her abuser. But not every survivor wants to face her perpetrator, and she shouldn't be forced to if she's not ready. Her healing doesn't hinge on a confrontation. But if confrontation is an important step to your survivor, she'll need your support. It's best not to try to talk her out of it.

She'll need to be psychologically prepared. Confrontation brings major emotional upheaval, and it doesn't always go as smoothly as we fantasize. In fact, it rarely does.

Facing my abuser—my dad—was essential for me. I wanted closure, but the first go around didn't bring closure at all. It slit me open and gutted me.

Looking back, I realize I didn't confront him correctly. I'm not blaming myself. His response was despicable. But I know now that my confrontation wasn't well planned. Truthfully, it wasn't planned at all.

I was spontaneous—I still am—and decided to pick up the phone and call.

"Dad, I want to forgive you for all the things you did to me as a child."

"What things?"

"You know, the way you touched me and hurt me."

"I don't know what you're talking about."

The conversation went downhill from there. After we hung up the phone, I sat, frozen. It seemed like hours, but only a few minutes passed when the phone rang again.

It was my dad.

Finally, he's going to confess. But it wasn't long before my hopes were dashed again. His confession didn't come that day.

"Hi, Dawnie. Listen, sweetheart, when we were talking earlier, your stepmother was on the other end of the phone. She misunderstood something you said. She thinks I've inappropriately touched you, you know, like sexually. Can you please clear it up for her? She needs to know I'm not a pedophile."

I was stunned. My dad wanted me to go along with this crazy scam. He called me, convinced I would cover his perverted actions. And why wouldn't I? I'd protected him for twenty-eight years.

He was right. My instincts were to guard the secret and protect him. *He's my dad and I love him,* I reasoned.

I mustered the strength to answer him.

"I'm sorry for the confusion, Dad. I'm not really sure what to say. Of course you're not a pedophile. Maybe we can talk about it later—in person."

That seemed to satisfy everyone.

Except me.

I was thrown back into the rage cycle. I was angry at a whole new level. This time every man in the world was going to pay for my father's crime. At that moment, Terry entered the room. He couldn't have picked a worse time to show up.

"What's wrong? You seem . . ."

"All you men do is lie. Every single one of you! There's not one honest man on this planet. I will *never* trust any of you." I blasted him with a torrent of fury.

My tirade was hurtful and totally misdirected. It wasn't fair. Terry knew not to take it personally, but I'm sure my behavior crushed him. Still, he came through for me.

"I'm sorry he hurt you, Dawn."

Some years later—maybe seven—my dad called me out of the blue. He wanted to come over and talk to me. I hung up the phone in disbelief.

Although we lived in the same city, he'd never been to my house. My son Tony was about four. My dad had seen him twice. My father and I didn't have much of a relationship.

My father arrived shortly after the call and asked if we could sit down in the living room. The memory is clearly etched in my mind.

"I want to tell you something. Remember when you called me years ago and told me you forgave me? I lied. I was afraid and I denied the truth. I know I hurt you. I hurt all of you girls. I have no explanation for my behavior. But if it's not too late, I'd like to be forgiven. I'm so sorry for what I put you through. I can't imagine how I've destroyed your life."

I swallowed hard. Hearing his words was surreal.

Can this really be happening? These are the words I've waited my whole life to hear.

"I forgive you, Dad. I forgave you a long time ago."

When I spoke the words of forgiveness, we both broke. I embraced my dad while we both wept bitterly. The tears washed our souls. I could feel the healing begin.

Then he spoke again.

"I look at you three daughters of mine and I think, 'Wow, I have the most incredible children.' You're all so talented and I'm so proud of you. But I have no relationship with you—for obvious reasons. I don't know who you are, or who you've become. I don't know my grandchildren. And I'm alone. I have everything anyone could want, but no one to share it with. I don't want to die a lonely old man. I want you back in my life. Is it too late? Is it even possible?"

It was a supernatural moment. God was with me. He gave me the grace to forgive.

After that day, my dad and I did enjoy the beginning stages of a new and beautiful relationship. But only a few short months into our fresh start, my dad was diagnosed with terminal cancer.

I was at his bedside when he breathed his last. So were my two sisters, my mother, and my brother-in-law. We held my dad's hands and sang to him as he was peacefully escorted into eternity. As we gathered in that room, I rested my eyes for a moment on each one present. My heart was soothed as I reflected back on my father's words, "I don't want to die a lonely old man."

In the final moments of my father's life, he wasn't alone, and he wasn't lonely. God's forgiveness was complete.

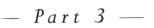
— *Part 3* —

HOW YOU
CAN HELP

FOSTERING A HEALING ENVIRONMENT

"I feel so safe and secure with my husband. I'm convinced that with his love and encouragement, I can look at the pain of my past without the fear of rejection or more abandonment. I really believe I can heal with him at my side." —Louise

She's endured a horrific childhood experience. For years, she's run from her pain in an attempt to avoid the gruesome truth. Until now.

Now she's found the strength to look at her abuse, uncover the shame, and deal with what's happened. But the looming question in her mind is, "Will I ever heal from this?"

Survivors can and do heal from sexual abuse. But feeling safe enough to let down our guard and begin the process is a major hurdle for many of us. While you're not responsible for her healing, you can validate her recovery in powerful ways.

I wanted to be free, but I was afraid to explore my healing with Terry as a support person. He was passive by nature and I realize now, I saw his passivity as more abuse. I knew he'd see me at my worst, and that worried me. *What if I completely unravel? He won't know what to do for me, and I won't be safe.* The prospect of becoming needy and vulnerable with him as my "first responder" threatened me.

Female survivors view passivity as abusive for several reasons. Passive supporters feel like supporters in word only to survivors. Since no one was there to rescue us from abuse, we look for actions to prove to us you care. That's why passivity hurts.

We need to be defended, and passive supporters often do nothing. We look for them to protect us, and they're often unavailable or unaware. We long to be comforted, but they're often silent—apparently at a loss for words. We need them to believe us, but they often question our recollections.

✦ ✦ ✦

The woman in your life has her own fears about healing. She'll probably test the temperature before she jumps into healing waters.

- Does she feel your love, support, and nurture?
- Can she let her walls down and allow you to see who she really is: broken and in need of love?
- Will she find you to be trustworthy?
- Can she discuss her abuse without being judged or dismissed?
- Can she find a confidant in you—someone who will listen, love, and understand?

The answers to these questions reveal the quality of her environment for healing. An affirmative response from you shows that a healing environment exists.

Remember, you can't *heal* her, but you can *help* her. The woman in your life is responsible for her own recovery. And you're responsible for your own well-being. But if you'll stand by her side and walk hand in hand, you'll both survive the recovery process.

Accept and Support

Now that you understand why she behaves the way she does, you're empowered to support her in a whole new way. While the goal is still for her to heal and be free from the fears and insecurities of her past, knowing what she has come through should give you fresh encouragement to accept her as she is.

Many of us grew up in a performance/reward system, and if that's true of the one you love, her tendency will be to continue to perform, even when she's hurting inside. She may also respond in the other extreme: acting like she doesn't care about anything and can't be motivated.

Either way, your unconditional love and acceptance provide the backdrop for her recovery, and beyond recovery, because at the end of her healing journey she'll still need unconditional love—she won't be perfect.

The writer Paul pens a beautiful treatise on perfect, unconditional love. Then suddenly in the midst of his discourse on love, he makes an important shift and refers to his childhood: "When I was a child, I talked like a child, I thought like a child, I reasoned like a child. When I became a man, I put childish ways behind me" (1 Cor. 13:11).

I've often wondered if a correlation existed to his becoming a man and unconditional love. Today, I'm convinced that correlation is important. An atmosphere of love is an important element of a growth environment. Healing, maturity, growth, and wholeness become a reality when love is present.

Paul says, "When I *became*."

The woman in your life is on her way to *becoming*. Your acceptance of her terrible past, the condition it left her in, and the journey ahead of the two of you will give her the support and safe atmosphere she needs to confidently pursue recovery. Your active support invigorates her. She needs more than just words; she needs to see them lived out.

There may be times when quite frankly, you will feel tired of the whole sexual abuse issue. I don't blame you. Recovery can be consuming. But she can't escape her journey—it's her reality. Your support, even when you're weary, nudges her toward wholeness.

When she needs to cry, offer your shoulder. If she has to vent, let your ear be her sounding board. Active support means listening, even when you'd rather be watching television.

When she's having an unusually bad day, you provide support when you say, "I'm here for you. Why don't you go and have some time alone? I'll get dinner ready."

At those times, you support her when you assert yourself and make the suggestion, "Why don't we take a walk and talk."

Listen

She was silent for a long time, pushing her secret deep inside. She may have talked about many other things, surface things. But most survivors don't share their pain, not with anyone. They don't even admit it to themselves.

So when she's ready to talk, listen. She needs to tell her story, and not just once. Most survivors share our past in bits and pieces. Maybe that's because we can't handle any more than that, and we're worried you can't either. But that's usually how our memories come back to us, in small random pieces. Each time we tell our story, it becomes clearer. We start to grasp the reality of what happened to us, this time not just with our heads. We believe and understand it with our hearts.

My friend Cecil Murphey said that in the early days of his recovery, he repeated things he'd said before as he told his story again and again. Once he stopped and apologized to the man he was speaking to, "You've heard this before."

"But you need to say it again," his friend reassured him.

Cecil said, "It gave me permission to tell my story as many times as I needed to."

She needs to talk to heal. Sensitive and engaged listening from you creates a safe place for her to divulge her most vulnerable secrets. When she's ready to, she'll open up. But don't force her, invite her. Let her know you're there to listen when she needs you. The more she talks, the more she becomes purged from the tender, emotional wound of her past.

One sign of healing came for me when I realized I could talk freely about my abuse without stabbing pain and anguish. I still feel compassion for myself and grieve over what was stolen from me, but I'm not raw and undone. I'm grateful to God for what he has brought me through.

Good listening is a skill that must be developed. A good listener draws out the speaker. Proverbs 20:5 says, "The purposes of a man's [*woman's*] heart are deep waters, but a man of understanding draws them out."

You'll know you're effectively listening when her words flow freely. This doesn't mean she's having an easy time sharing her story, but it means she finds you safe and comforting to talk to.

Poor listening skills usually reflect selfishness or ignorance. The listener either doesn't want to hear what's being said, or they aren't aware that their listening style is ineffective.

A survivor can immediately detect poor listening. You may be ineffectively listening if she shuts down and refuses to open up. Her flow of words becomes clogged, and it may take awhile for her to open up and build trust again.

Listening That Draws

Give her your undivided attention.

Let your eye contact and body language say, "Nothing is more important right now than you and what you're telling me."

Once she starts sharing, don't interrupt her. Don't multi-task with your computer and phone while she's talking. Turn the TV off and focus on her. Be careful not to yawn. You may not mean to communicate disinterest, but these are all signals that say, "I don't care." Or, "I'm not really interested in you."

Accept what she tells you without judgment.

Her story may seem unbelievable, sketchy, or the details may be different from the last time she told it. Don't correct her. Just listen. She's working through her memories. Even if the specifics aren't accurate, her feelings are real. The more she talks, the clearer her experience becomes.

Nonjudgmental listening permits her story to unfold. It takes amazing courage for her to share. She's telling you the most intimate and shameful parts of her life.

She's watching you along the way, looking for the slightest hint of disapproval or negative reaction. If she senses these things, she'll retreat and take her secret with her.

When you accept what she tells you without moral judgments or condemning statements, you tell her she's safe with you.

Validate her.

You facilitate her sharing when you respond to her stories with compassion and empathy. Your response doesn't have to be eloquent to be meaningful. You can say, "I hurt for you." When you say, "I'm sorry you went through so much pain," you give her permission to grieve for herself.

Validation tells the survivor she's a strong and beautiful woman. You can simply say, "You've made it through an incredible trauma. I'm proud of you."

She may fear that once she shares her experience, she'll be rejected. The secret shame she's carried leads her to believe she's flawed beyond repair. Now that you know about her past, she may wonder if you'll still love and support her.

When you validate her you soothe her fear.

Don't be afraid of silence.

One of the most powerful moments of healing came when I stopped talking.

The precious woman I had been counseling for several months was still stuck. Week after week I offered Sherry my best advice, prayed with her, and gave her scriptures. But nothing seemed to be helping. She wasn't getting anywhere, and I was exhausted from trying to heal her.

When Sherry came one Wednesday, I shot up a quick prayer. "Jesus, you have to do something. I'm out of ideas." That's when I heard his response, "Then be quiet. I'll take over."

I opened in prayer and then told Sherry, "Today I want to hear from you."

For the next twenty-five minutes we sat in total silence. Sherry, in trance-like meditation, stared at the floor, almost without blinking. Everything inside of me was screaming, *Lord, are you sure this is going to work? It's been nearly thirty minutes.*

Seconds later Sherry spoke. Soft and gentle, her trembling voice broke the silence.

"Does God love me?"

Aware of the sacredness of the moment, I was afraid to speak. I nodded yes.

"But is he mad at me?"

Still quiet, I shook my head no.

That's when the floodgates opened. Sherry cried bitter tears for several minutes. Her breakthrough had finally come. And it was ushered in on the wings of silence.

I learned an important lesson that day. Sometimes silence is the only appropriate answer.

Listening That Clogs

Don't try to fix her.

Men and women are wired differently. Often women tend to pour out their hearts while their husbands look for ways to solve the problem. When the survivor in your life mulls over her past, she's not looking for a solution, she's looking to vent.

Resist the temptation to rush in with advice-giving and problem-solving techniques. If you say, "Well, if you want to get better, I think you should . . ." you take the risk of shutting down her transparency.

Instead, try asking reflective questions:

+ "What do you think you should do?"
+ "What do you want to do?"
+ "What are you feeling right now?"

Effective listening helps her draw her own conclusions. She's empowered and more apt to follow through when she's discovered her own solution.

Don't minimize her pain.

Be careful not to comfort her with shallow words:

+   "Oh, you'll be okay."
+   "It's in the past now. Let it go."

Or worse, never question the severity of her abuse and its impact on her:

+   "Was it really that bad?"
+   "Don't overreact."

Before my husband realized the massive impact of sexual abuse on victims, he said, "What happened to you wasn't so bad. I've heard of much worse. Besides, it happened a long time ago. You should be over it by now." I wasn't.

When she tells you how she feels, believe her. She trusts you with her soul. Be careful not to betray that trust.

Don't overreact.

Perhaps this is the first time you've heard her story. Don't overreact. Your overreaction could add to the anxiety she already feels. Your extreme reaction may also hinder her from talking to you. Try not to act shocked or display too much anger. You want to be supportive, and it's important to show a demonstrative response. But an overresponse can backfire with a survivor. She may feel more shame if she sees how vile her experience is to you.

Lay-leaders from my church desiring to become prayer partners are trained to become "shock-proof." To help them understand what I mean, we role-play. I present them with graphic stories while they practice listening. They monitor their reactions and respond with positive and soothing tones and comments.

You may want to practice, too. Prepare yourself to be calm, compassionate, and supportive.

Reassuring phrases such as "I'm so sorry for the betrayal you've experienced" or, "I certainly understand how you would feel that way," validate her feelings.

The Value of Friendship

She needs you to be her trusted ally.

The survivor has difficulty maintaining meaningful friendships because of the tendency to withdraw from others during the healing process. But she needs a close and trustworthy friend.

You support her in a powerful way when you choose to be a friend that says, "I'm here for you" or, "If you want to be alone, I understand." "I'm here to help you in any way I can."

Friendship includes many benefits:

- Sharing and telling secrets
- Doing nothing together
- Taking walks or going out to coffee
- Carrying each other's burdens
- Praying for one another
- Supporting one another

Friends care for each other. It helps her to be your friend, too. Let her know what your needs are when it's the right time.

And remind her that you care for her. You can't heal her, but you can stand by her side.

Respect Boundaries

Remember her life was invaded. She was violated, her personal boundaries trampled on and ignored. Now she's exploring what it means to have healthy boundaries. She wonders what's appropriate in setting boundaries and if she has the *right* to implement them.

Do I deserve to be respected?

The real question is whether she'll respect herself enough to enforce healthy, sound personal boundaries. You can help her by showing her that she's worthy of her own space and privacy.

A woman who has been dishonored needs to know that she has the power of choice. She can say *no* and not be rejected, or she can say *yes* and not be ashamed. At first, she may be confused about what's acceptable, since she's spent most of her life with broken and blurred boundaries.

I didn't understand the whole boundary thing at first. My best friend Laurie was going through her own healing journey (not related to sexual abuse). She'd often share the new insights she was learning along the way. When she began to talk about "setting a boundary" with certain people, I wasn't sure what she meant. She explained, "Setting a boundary means I have the right to accept or not accept certain treatment from others. I don't have to roll over and play dead just because someone wants their way. I can choose."

My initial reaction was, "How can you do that? You'll lose all your friends."

It was a risky move as far as I was concerned and something I would've never considered. Not with people I cared for and admired anyway.

I can say no to people? I can draw lines and say you can only come this far into my life?

I'd assumed if someone wanted something from me they could take it. If they asked me a probing question, I should answer, even if I was uncomfortable. If someone had unmet needs, I must meet them. My needs were of no consequence.

Then one day I was watching television and ran across a show, something similar to *This Old House*. An antiquated, historic Victorian home was being restored. The house was beautiful and well worth saving, although the transformation was complex and involved. The show was nearly over, the renovation almost complete, when the last scene took us viewers to a secret attic entrance. The cameras were rolling as the crew entered the mysterious room.

Once inside the attic, the builders uncovered what seemed to be a pile of useless metal. After further inspection, the renovators became ecstatic. They'd discovered the original fence for the property. They were thrilled at their finding and estimated the value of the house had increased dramatically because they'd recovered a fence that could be restored.

The parallel was clear to me. I needed boundaries in my life to restore me to God's original design. Fences in my life would also protect my God-given value.

The woman in your life needs to build boundaries, too. The process may seem awkward at first and the pendulum may swing from one extreme to the other, as she chooses few boundaries or severely rigid ones. But as she becomes more confident in her progress, she will develop the kind of healthy boundaries God intends for her.

Establish Your Boundaries

Rebuilding boundaries is essential for abuse survivors. But establishing boundaries for you, the man, is also vital. Some husbands are tempted to help their wives recover by yielding to their every desire and decision. Husbands often become passive peacekeepers who allow their wives to have their way, even if it means the men become doormats. Although the passive peacekeeper's goal may be love, support, and sometimes survival, his goals—and hers—are better served by creating and maintaining healthy boundaries.

Seeing her husband model healthy boundaries does more for a wife in recovery than seeing him bend to please her. When she observes her husband's loving determination and self-respect, she learns what it means to be whole and to respect boundaries.

You can best help your wife as you build and maintain your own healthy boundaries. The healthiest of marriages are those between husbands and wives that find the balance between caring for each other's needs and maintaining sound and responsible personal boundaries.

Since you love her, you want to please her. Although that's important, you have needs, too. If you ignore your feelings during her healing, you won't help your wife or your marriage, and you may both end up dealing with additional resentment and anger.

— *26* —

UNDERSTANDING HER NEED TO CONTROL

"I admit it. I'm a control freak. But what's so bad about that? I just like to know what's going to happen next." —Iris

As a child she had no control. She lost her voice and was stripped of power. Her boundaries were violated and her world careened out of control. Life was chaotic, and she was afraid.

Now in an attempt to regain sanity, a woman with an abusive past is desperate to manage the reins of power over her environment. She often becomes a controller. Anyone would. Controlling behavior is the hallmark of many people who've experienced frightening and tumultuous childhoods.

Ironically, a survivor's need for control can become a compulsion. They become addicted to the false sense of security that power and control bring. I say "false sense" because control creates an illusion. She may feel that as long as she holds the reins, she's safe from pain. But freedom from life's hurtful experiences doesn't pass us by, no matter how much control we wield.

In order for a woman to experience authentic healing, she needs to discover a healthy balance in expressing control. She has to take risks and relinquish some of the things she tries to control. That word alone—*relinquish*—sends a panic through most survivors. But because control is a cover-up for brokenness, she won't know how complete her healing is until she's willing to let go of inappropriate power and control.

That's a difficult thing to do.

For one reason, many survivors don't recognize their patterns of control. This powerful defense mechanism—like many of the others—has become second nature. If she's open to your suggestions, you can help her identify some of the ways she exerts control.

Surrendering control makes her feel dangerously vulnerable. She feels helpless and powerless, and those feelings trigger other painful emotions similar to the fear and doom she felt in childhood.

Control feels logical and the only tried-and-true way to ease paralyzing emotions.

Dominance as a Form of Control

Some survivors view control as "winning." They don't just want to simply exert control, they seek to dominate, and they do so in the following ways:

Conversation

Remember, *winning* is important. She may be a debater or disputer. She may be a pouter and stonewaller. She may scream and rage and use intimidation, but at the end of every conversation, she gets her way. Controlling the conversation—the content, the direction, the length, and the outcome—is her attempt to feel powerful.

Food

Since the survivor had no control as a child, she can rule by the way she eats. Food is a major source of power for any survivor. Many have said, "I can control what I eat and how much I eat, and no one can take it away from me." Food is also one way we self-soothe.

Children

Survivors often flex their manipulative muscles by exerting influence and control over their children. They may vacillate between being the over-dominating parent or the permissive, "I-want-to-be-your-best-friend" parent.

Many women vicariously relive their childhoods through their children. They force their kids into activities, social groups, sports, and events that will make them feel popular. They especially control their daughters in the area of appearance.

Money

Survivors also express control in the way they spend money. They often construct and enforce rigid financial budgets. They give allowances, make financial decisions, and closely monitor expenditures.

Yet with all that power, it's not uncommon for survivors to vacillate between extremes on this subject also. They may impose financial demands on their families and excuse themselves from the strict parameters of the budget. Some survivors spend money to ease internal conflicts, while others hoard money to enhance their sense of security.

Sex

Most survivors of sexual assault have a strong need to control the sexual area of their lives. Because sex is associated with pain and trauma, the conditions of a sexual encounter have to be just right.

Sex stirs up gut-wrenching emotions, so don't be surprised when she tries to avoid intimacy. She's likely to squash any sexual connection she didn't initiate. And she seldom initiates.

Relationships

It's natural to want to manage our lives, but the woman with control issues attempts to exert her influence over everyone around her, too.

Debbie, a survivor, admitted, "I'm a control freak. I have a need to be in control of everything and everyone around me."

Passivity as a Form of Control

Not every survivor's pain is expressed in obvious ways. Outward displays of anger, controlling behaviors, and defense mechanisms may not describe the one in your life. That's because some survivors are passive survivors. When life became overwhelming, the passive survivor retreated through emotional slumber. She's supine—lying flat on her back on the inside, drained of life.

Passive survivors often use these kinds of phrases to define themselves:

"I'm a walking dead woman."

"I do things and go places, but inside, my soul is withered and dry."

"There's no life in me."

Lethargic, apathetic, listless, and lifeless: if these words describe the one you love, she may still be slumbering—she's not fully awake to life.

A survivor's passiveness becomes a source of control. Her inactivity manipulates others around her. They feel responsible *for* her and accountable *to* her. In this way, she has successfully assured herself that she is in control of those around her.

Your Response to Her Control

Don't cave in.

You can support her by understanding her control issues but not caving in to them. She wants to be in the power position and sometimes that's okay and appropriate. But when it's not and it's a violation of your boundaries, you help her best by maintaining a strong, healthy commitment to your personal convictions. You don't need to get into a power struggle with her. Remember, the root of her control issue is fear. She lost her "voice" as a child, and she's afraid it could happen again. She needs to be able to express her thoughts and desires. But a loving, patient, yet firm resolve from you will help her redirect her focus to look within herself to settle her anxieties instead of trying to control externals.

Help her identify control.

Some survivors are oblivious to the ways they control. Others aren't and readily admit to their control issues. But if she's willing, you can help the woman who's not fully aware of how she's expressing control. Ask her if she wants to overcome her habit. If she's ready and willing, then take the opportunity to gently point out her controlling behavior. I'm not suggesting for a moment that this is easy. Shifting control away from a survivor is like removing the pacifier from a distraught infant. It's going to be messy. But if she trusts you have her best interest at heart, she'll be more open to listen when you tell her she's using control as a means to cope.

Don't ignore red flags.

Some forms of her control can be innocent—albeit very irritating and frustrating—but they're not necessarily dangerous to her or others. Pay attention to the red flags, however, and be careful that the control tactics your survivor uses don't become damaging or abusive to those around her.

Potentially threatening control behaviors could include

- ✦ Irrational, raging, or angry behavior
- ✦ Physical displays: hitting, severe spanking, pushing, shoving
- ✦ Verbal abuse: yelling, screaming, name calling
- ✦ Withdrawal of love, open rejection of family
- ✦ Shutting down emotionally, unresponsiveness
- ✦ Using silence, starvation, or isolation
- ✦ Using intimidation or bullying children; restricting activities, excessive grounding
- ✦ Emotional abuse
- ✦ Parental inversion: demanding the child parent her

If you see these signs, then you should consider getting professional help. Seeking counsel for you and for her may be the only way to deactivate a potential time bomb and keep it from exploding.

✦   ✦   ✦

When the adult survivor recognizes that she's no longer a defenseless child, susceptible to hurt and assault, she's more likely to release the control she wields. The process is part of the healing journey, and at the end she won't be perfect. Walking through the process of releasing control will take time and intentionality.

— 27 —

BUILDING TRUST IN SEXUAL INTIMACY

"It's taken us some time—a long time. But we're starting to really connect.
Our lovemaking is so much deeper now that we're working together." —Larry

You may face moments when you wonder, "Will she ever enjoy sex again?" It's a fair question, and the answer is different for every survivor. But I can assure you, a good sex life won't materialize on its own.

Terry and I stumbled over many obstacles in trying to find the "Emerald City" of lovemaking. We fell short of the glorious destination by about two million miles. I was wounded, and he was stubborn, and that combination led to a dead-end on the road to sexual recovery.

It's possible for you to do better.

Sexual intimacy is the glue that God gives marriage partners to bond hearts together. In no other union is such a magnificent closeness and intimacy formed. Yet at the same time, no other force is as powerfully destructive and painful as sexual perversion.

Since you love her, take time with her. If you'll nurture your sexual life, you'll have a much better hope of reaching a wonderfully satisfying sexual relationship.

✦   ✦   ✦

During the healing process, most women despise sexual urges or impulses. She abruptly shuts them down. She negatively associates those feelings with one of the most horrible experiences of her life. You can understand why she wouldn't want to be reminded of it.

Think of it this way. Imagine you've just had dinner at a local restaurant. Soon after you eat, you become violently sick, and you lose your stomach. It's the flu. But you can't stop from making a connection between what you've just eaten and the feelings of being sick. The association is made. The next time you go into that same restaurant, you involuntarily become nauseous. You can't stay; you lose your appetite, and you want to leave.

Many women feel this way after they've been sexually abused. The event is so traumatic that survivors often have an involuntarily violent reaction to being sexually stimulated.

In building trust with you, the woman you love can learn in a safe environment how to separate her negative associations. Her repulsion needs to be directed toward her abuser and the abuse, not toward you and sexual intimacy.

Learning to aim her pain in the proper direction takes specific focus. Her tendency may be to project her negative feelings about sex on you. It can happen quickly during lovemaking. At those times, gently remind her that you love her and she's safe with you. You can ask her, "What did I do just now to trigger you?"

If she tells you what she doesn't like, you've become empowered to avoid certain behaviors and actions that resemble her abuse. It's better for you to adjust your style than to force her to accept the action. Pushing her to like something that simulates her abuse experience will simply feel like more abuse to her. In making the shift in your behavior, you prove your love and your trustworthiness and that you're not at all like her abuser.

Trust is the key in building sexual intimacy. If she can trust you as a sensitive and gentle lover, she may learn how to open herself up and allow herself to be free. Her trust for you implies important things: You'll stop when she says no. You'll change what you're doing if she says, "I don't like that." It means you won't reject her if she does say no. If she touches you, you'll assure her that it feels good and she's doing it right. This is the kind of trust and safety she needs.

✦   ✦   ✦

I desperately wanted trust in my relationship. Once I discovered why I was struggling with intimacy—that lack of trust was a side effect from sexual abuse—I wanted to overcome my fears. I asked for the things I thought would help me to break through. But Terry dismissed my requests.

"I'm not cracking a safe here. And I'm not going to learn some combination. Besides, you'll change tomorrow anyway."

He may have been right; I might have changed the entry code. I was learning what worked, too. But I knew one thing for sure: what we were doing wasn't working. After twenty-seven years of chasing the wind, he ended our marriage.

I suggest the following components in your relationship to build sexual intimacy. Perhaps you can read the ideas together and see if she agrees. They can help you reach a new place of freedom.

Talking About Your Sex Life

It's important to talk about your sexual life. But even talking about the sensitive area of sex can be dangerous territory. It might work best if you approach the subject in a safe and neutral environment where she's certain sexual intimacy will not follow. Sharing in a quiet corner of a coffee shop or sitting on a park bench is usually nonthreatening, and she'll be more likely to let her guard down.

Talk to her about your desire to have a healthy sexual life, and share with her what that life would look like for you. Ask her if she shares that desire and find out what a fulfilling sex life would look like for her. Communicating about these things in a gentle and highly sensitive way can promote tremendous healing for you both and build mutual trust. It's important to know if you share the same goals for your intimate life.

You can ask the following kinds of questions:

+ What do you enjoy?
+ Where do you like to be touched?
+ Are there things I should avoid?
+ What time and place works best for you?

+ What doesn't work for you?
+ What is your idea of a fulfilling sexual encounter?
+ What should I know about you?

You can also add to your trust and intimacy by letting her know you care about her experience. You can simply say, "Help me understand what you've been through so I know what to do for you."

Good, clear, and nonjudgmental communication is a top priority in building sexual trust.

Not Forcing Your Will on Hers

Her abuse can be summed up as one survivor put it, "He pushed his will onto mine and stole from me."

That's not your intention, but at times she may feel forced. Because someone stole from her, having a voice in your sexual intimacy is critical for her. She desires to be a ready participant, not taken against her will.

That means she doesn't want you to use manipulation, guilt, or rejection to persuade her to perform. Coercion may get your needs met on Saturday night, but come Sunday morning you'll be faced with her anger, tears, rage, and rejection. When that happens, no one wins, and the chasm between you grows wider.

She needs to trust you in intimacy as much or more than she does anywhere.

"Will he still love me if I say no?" The woman you love needs to know if you'll be patient and understanding if she's not open to sex or if, instead, she'll receive the brunt of your anger.

Helping Her Accept Her Body

Many survivors are body-shy. They are awkward about their bodies and don't have full command over them. Some women feel clumsy; they walk hunched over or aren't fluid in their movements. They're self-conscious, and their body language communicates it: "Don't notice me."

Body-shyness is another result of sexual abuse. Being uncovered and exposed as children leaves many women feeling shameful and uncomfortable with their bodies. These feelings of shame are magnified in the context of sexual intimacy.

Karen, a woman in my recovery group for sexual abuse survivors, had a perfectly sculpted body. She was beautiful, yet I wasn't surprised when she told me, "On my honeymoon night, I hid in the bathroom for fifteen minutes. I couldn't bring myself to show my husband my body. I cracked the door open and called out to him to turn the lights off. Everything had to be pitch-black before I could come out."

Most women are unsatisfied in some way with their bodies to begin with, but adding the scar of sexual abuse exacerbates the issue. Be aware that she's listening and watching you for cues about how you feel about her body. Even a playful comment about her size, shape, or weight can send her into rejection. Survivors often find it difficult to hear innocent or teasing remarks. Those comments are filtered through the distortions of her past. The message she may hear is that she's ugly and physically disgusting to you. Secretly, that's how she often feels about herself.

Your words, gestures, and actions are valuable to her. You can help her tackle body-shyness by showing her that she's beautiful and appealing. Be generous in your verbal expressions. Tell her, "I love the way you look. You're beautiful to me." Don't be put off if at first she deflects your compliments. She probably will. Remember, your words confront lies planted deep in her soul that tell her she's unbecoming and, therefore, unacceptable and unlovable.

If you'll remain diligent in blessing her with affirmation, she'll most likely learn to accept what you say as truth. As her confidence builds, she's more apt to abandon her fears and give herself to you more fully.

Helping Her Accept Touch

The survivor also heals as she learns to reclaim the ability to give touch and receive touch.

Most survivors have acute senses. We're extremely sensitive to smell, sound, words, facial expressions, and touch. We react quickly and often negatively to those cues. We often need to be desensitized from potentially negative touch triggers. You can help her become comfortable with touch through nonsexual physical touch or touch that promises not to become sexually stimulating. Couples can work together to create intimacy by practicing nurturing touch. Holding hands, cuddling and hugging, gently massaging and stroking one another are all ways to learn and explore the wonders of each other.

I've talked with countless women who have all shared a common dream. They really do want to have the courage to explore their husband's body without being taken over by his sexual aggression. Even if a man becomes aroused, she doesn't need to become defensive when she trusts he will not act on his desire. Passionate lovemaking is the eventual goal, but right now she's reclaiming her ability to touch and be touched.

Avoiding Surprises

Sexual abuse survivors need to know what to expect, especially during a sexual encounter. Simply put, survivors don't like surprises when it comes to sex.

You can help build trust if she knows what you're going to do during sexual intimacy. You can add to your lovemaking experience and build anticipation if you say to her, "I want to touch you here." Tell her what you'd like to do and move slowly, even though this approach may seem mechanical at first.

Be gentle. Don't pull and push her. Tenderly stroke and caress her, and don't be afraid to speak softly. Women are verbal in the same way men are visual.

Letting Her Initiate

One of the carryovers from abuse for female survivors is in the area of initiating sex. Many women find it particularly difficult to assert themselves. This isn't necessarily because she doesn't desire to initiate or have sex, but one reason may be because she's ashamed to admit she's having sexual urges.

Another reason why she doesn't initiate in intimate relations is often due to her perception of an *initiator*. Because she's accustomed to being forced for sexual stimulation, she may feel like an abuser when she asserts herself. Because of conflicting feelings and confusion, she'd rather avoid initiating altogether than struggle to sort out her feelings.

Let her know if you'd enjoy her initiating sexual intimacy. Give her permission to approach you and share with her in what ways initiating would work best for you. Learn what initiating looks like from her so you don't miss her cues and accidentally reject her. Many abused women are sensitive and hesitant when it comes to sexuality, let alone being the sexual aggressor.

Some women, however, are very aggressive. The woman you love may have a sexual drive that's very strong. It's not uncommon for the pendulum to swing to either extreme. The main focus is to make sure your sexual experience is an expression of the true intimacy you share in your relationship. Not sharing sex is frustrating and hurtful. If she demands extreme amounts of sex, you may wonder if she's connected emotionally and capable of a deeper intimacy.

True intimacy is the goal.

Working Together

You have to pay for the actions of another, and it's not fair. But the woman you love is a survivor of the most hurtful and intimate invasion possible. And although it's her problem, you love her and are in an intimate relationship with her. You're an important part of her life. If you want to connect with her at the deepest level, her abusive past becomes your problem, too.

Unfortunately, some spouses live the motto, "Ignore it and it will go away." You may have been tempted to feel that way, too. Many men would rather ignore their loved one's abuse and hope that the effects of her unspeakable sexual history will go away. But sexual trauma seldom, if ever, dissipates.

Together you'll have to work through the snares of sexual abuse, but the rewards can be extremely gratifying. The healing journey will draw you closer as you build an intimate, trusting, and fulfilling sexual bond.

— *28* —

PRAYING FOR HER

"Again, I tell you that if two of you on earth agree about anything you ask for, it will be done for you by my Father in heaven. For where two or three come together in my name, there am I with them." —Jesus (Matt. 18:19–20)

Little else is more powerful than petitioning God in prayer. His divine strength and guidance is needed for your journey.

Pray aloud for her.

God's Word says, "The prayer of a righteous man is powerful and effective" (James 5:16). God hears your prayers, and he answers them. She can benefit from hearing them, too. Although she may not be able to articulate her prayers in front of you, your prayers for her and *over* her can bring her closer to God's healing. When you pray out loud for her, her faith is encouraged. Prayer gives us the hope to believe in a better future, one that's filled with peace and wholeness.

I've been tremendously impacted by hearing someone formulate words, entreating the God of all wisdom, just for me. In the midst of some very dark days, I've felt the Lord's comfort lift me up.

If you can, pray aloud in her presence each day. The Holy Spirit will be faithful to lead you to ways to pray for her.

Pray for her complete inner healing.

One significant prayer for a survivor is to ask that God will restore the years that have been stolen from her through child abuse. Ask that his healing rebuild the child within and help the undeveloped areas of her personality reach maturity.

Pray for her renewed self-esteem.

She also needs prayer for her self-esteem and worth. An abused woman's view of herself is often severely distorted. As she learns to claim and apply the truth about her intrinsic value and worth, lies and old messages will fall away. Pray that she will claim what God says about her—that she's valuable, chosen by him, loveable, forgivable, and worthy of a great and special future. Your prayers help her hear the truth about who she is.

Reassure her of your prayers.

In addition to praying aloud for her, let her know you will continue to pray for her whenever God impresses you to do so. Telling her, "I prayed for you today" can give her a sense of trust and partnership. Your words will say to her, "I care about you. You're not alone."

◆   ◆   ◆

You create an umbrella of safety for the woman you love with your prayers. She's going through a vulnerable and emotional experience as she journeys the healing path. She'll battle depression, fear, anxiety, and a host of other emotional hazards.

Recovering from sexual abuse is a time of spiritual war, and she dare not fight alone. Prayer is a powerful weapon that can build a wall of protection around her. She will take greater strides toward healing when she realizes she can let down her defenses and embrace the healing process without fear.

You're standing with her in prayer. God is for her. With that knowledge and loving prayer support, she can abandon her fear and journey forward.

29

SHE NEEDS YOU

"His steadiness was the foundation that kept me moving forward. So many times I screamed to quit and he would just embrace me and confirm his faith in me." —Kathy

She needs you. More than she knows or wants to believe.

Many adult survivors endeavor to be independent and self-sufficient. In admitting to our vulnerability and neediness, we risk more pain and rejection. Yet in remaining withdrawn and isolated, we do more than risk. We ensure our broken, wounded condition will continue. In the safety of your love, she can take a leap of faith and press on.

And she'll need support from you to help her.

Your Positive Attitude about Her Recovery

Your optimistic outlook will help her move more quickly through her healing. If she feels the need to say, "I'm sorry," it may mean she still feels guilty about being a sexual abuse victim. Remind her, "It's not your fault."

Let her know you love her as she is, and you're honored to be the one walking by her side. Then follow through and accept her as she is. Even after her healing journey is over, she'll have her own eccentricities and eclectic style of living.

Your Honesty About What You're Feeling

She wants to know how you feel. Don't lie or try to hide your feelings from her. She'll sniff you out. We women are notorious for taking the "temperature" of the one we love. If you're troubled, angry, weary, disappointed, and/or frustrated, she'll sense something is wrong. Be honest. Tell her how you're feeling and what you're experiencing. Your honesty will help her remember she's not the only one going through a challenging time. The healing process is demanding of you, too. It's healthy for her to get her eyes off of herself for a while and care for your needs. Be gentle and sensitive. But let her see your emotional state. Your transparency gives her permission to be transparent, too. She can learn how to accept her emotions when she sees how you process what you're feeling.

Let's say the woman you love just had a difficult encounter with her boss, and you were present to hear their conversation. You can turn that negative event into a growing moment by saying, "It hurt me when he spoke to you disrespectfully. I could see the confusion on your face. How are you feeling about what he said?" In that simple way, sharing your emotions can help her to explore and admit to her own.

Your Patience

Respect her pace, and don't push her toward goals she's not ready for. It's critical for you both to create realistic expectations. If she sees that you're overeager for her to recover, she may revert to concealing her issues and, instead, put on a false front of recovery. Her "pretending" is reinforced if she gains your approval for "getting over the past."

Be patient. Change is possible, and it will happen, but let her move through healing at her own speed. If you see her trying to cover over or minimize her woundedness, encourage her to remain open to the full healing process. There are no shortcuts on the road to recovery. I often heard the words, "You should be healed by now. It happened so long ago. Don't you think it's time to let go of it?" Those words may have been meant to cheer me on, but they actually convinced me that no one understood my deep wound. They were one more reminder that I faced my healing alone.

Your Fair Perspective

Some of the issues in your relationship are directly connected to her abusive past, but not all of them. Be careful not to blame her sexual abuse for everything that goes wrong. You have a history that needs to be understood, too. Together, you both bring experiences—happy and painful—into your marriage. She's probably made many mistakes, but help her know you understand that she's been coping the best way she knows how. Be honest about the areas of struggle that are part of your personal history and pain and tell her about your triggers.

Your Flexibility

By now you're more aware than anyone that living with a survivor can be a roller-coaster ride. Her emotions go up and down as she moves through the phases of healing. One minute she needs your arms wrapped around her, and the next minute she says, "I need some space." She may be sexually alive and open to a night of romance and lovemaking, then she's cold and unresponsive to your touch. She can be tough and impenetrable, and then she cries easily because, "You looked at me funny." You're riding the wave with her and probably getting seasick. But your flexible and understanding spirit make it possible for her to flow through the vacillating currents—a common part of the healing process—without fear of repercussions. Most days she doesn't understand her moods either. Her wide-ranging responses are all a natural part of working her way through the matrix of recovery. She's used to shutting off her pain and dissociating from intense emotion. But now she's allowing feelings to emerge, naturally and without suppression. If you're rigid and unbending, you'll both encounter stress and anxiety.

Your Commitment

Her world was threatening and uncertain. Adults who were supposed to love and protect her betrayed her. Friends who said they'd support and accept her have become weary and neglected her. She's been exploited, uncovered, raped, abandoned, and humiliated. To a woman who's been stripped and degraded by abuse, it's a terrifying thought to live through more rejection or abandonment. She's reluctant to open up her heart and receive love. Instead of releasing herself to a trusting and transparent relationship, a female survivor is more inclined to protect her heart and live within the confines of her self-made, isolated, safety zone. She may or may not know it, but she's keeping her emotional guard up, distancing herself from intimacy and closeness.

But your sincere commitment can change that. The commitment, security, and trust you provide give her the freedom to face her past. She's probably afraid because she understands that pursuing wholeness and healing begins with her undoing the system of protection she's always known.

She knows it will probably get worse before it gets better. Embracing her past is going to feel chaotic. She's descending into the basement of her soul to open up every tightly packed box she's ever hidden away. She feels she is regressing in her healing, trying to believe that facing the pain of her abuse will lead her to wholeness.

If she trusts you to stand with her, to love her in spite of what you might see, to withhold judgment and criticism of her glaring flaws, then she'll take the risk of her undoing to pursue her healing.

Your woman needs you. If you've got staying power and commit your love to her through the journey, her healing will accelerate. Your bond of intimacy will grow and be strengthened.

✦   ✦   ✦

I asked some precious friends of mine who are also survivors—some just starting in their healing process—what they needed from their partners. Here's what they said:

Becca

I cried out often for reassurance and love. I couldn't love myself, and it was hard to accept that someone else could love me. I felt so unworthy of anyone's love.

But the thing my husband did that helped was to let me vent and take me in his arms and assure me that he would not ever leave me. I tried to get him to reject me to prove my unworthiness of his love. I couldn't make him leave, for he'd made a commitment to God and to me. He never gave up on me.

However, looking back and knowing what I know now, I think if he'd prayed with me and had done spiritual warfare against the Enemy while I was feeling low and angry, that would have helped more than anything and would have helped bring healing faster.

Having said that, in reality, my husband could only show me the love of Jesus (and he did). But he could not make me receive forgiveness and love from God. But he loved me long enough that I became convinced of God's love for me, for I saw it and felt it in my husband's love for me. God healed my heart through my husband's constant and faithful love for me.

Krista

My husband could do three things for me.

One was not make his happiness depend on me. I needed him to be in a good mood, even when I wasn't, and not blame me for him feeling bad or unloved. Two, I needed him to be understanding about my unwillingness to be intimate.

Three, my heart was so shattered, I just frankly needed space. I was struggling with hating my husband, and it seemed every little thing he did just made the pain more intense. When a wound is still raw, even the slightest touch sends the patient reeling.

Catherine

In preparing to marry my husband, I was as honest with him as I could be about being abused as a child. I openly expressed to him as much as I remembered at the time. My knowledge was incomplete because I had buried the details in the depths of my mind and heart. In telling him about my abuse, I was trying to disclose that I needed him to be an understanding, tender, compassionate person and lover who cared about my feelings and allowed me to set boundaries because of my fears of being controlled. Those were not the words I spoke to him, but it was the cry of my heart. Every part of me wanted him to understand I needed him to love and accept me as a whole person and try to understand where I was coming from without seeing me as damaged. And I desperately needed my husband to demonstrate self-control—not to be forceful or demanding.

When the details of my past finally surfaced and I began to seek healing, I needed him to stand beside me unwaveringly and hold me tight, yet give me space. I needed him to discern when to hold me and when to give me space. I needed room to breathe on my own, and at other times I needed to be securely in his arms without feeling condemned. I needed him to simply be there for me—to love me, listen to me, and walk with me without being irritated as my life spiraled up and down. As I walked toward healing, I needed him to realize he could not be the person in my life holding me accountable for my changes. I needed him to be patient and forgive me for the many times I lost control as my wounds were healing. In hindsight, I now see I needed much more from him than I could give in return.

Candi

I needed my husband to love me unconditionally. Not to leave me, even if I told him to go away. I needed him to try to understand where I was at, and know me well enough to read between the lines when I wasn't making sense because the emotions took over. No easy feat.

What I needed most was for him to listen to my story, hear my pain, validate my experiences, and reassure me that he would always love me and never leave me. This touches some raw emotions. He did these things, and I am so blessed. I'm continually in awe that God cares enough about me to have brought my husband into my life.

✦   ✦   ✦

She needs you.

Your survivor wants to take the journey with you by her side. The more you encourage her, the more strength she'll draw for her healing.

30

AND WHAT ABOUT YOU?

"I want to love and support her. But does she want to do the same for me? It seems like everything is all about her. What about me?" —Dave

It's been a rough day. Your boss is at your throat, deadlines are looming, pressure is mounting, and you're ready to snap. You can't wait to get home, relax, and soak in some tender, loving care from the woman you love.

But when you arrive, your survivor is crying. She's had a bad day, too. "Get ready," you tell yourself. You take a deep breath, dismiss your needs, and seek to console and comfort your partner. Once again, you've been trumped; her pain takes precedence over yours.

She's not trying to out-do you on purpose. But something triggered her, and she's working though a torturous memory. The same thing happened last week, too. You put your needs aside to care for her.

Sound familiar?

Living with a survivor can mean facing many grueling days. The road to recovery is demanding and sometimes exhausting. You'll watch her go through agony as she sorts out her tumultuous past. She'll experience an array of emotions, and you'll experience them along with her. You're both making a gut-wrenching journey.

You're walking this intense path together, so it's important for you to realize she's not the only one who needs support. You'll need understanding and help, too. Your feelings may manifest in unpredictable ways. If you're going to stay effective in your support role, you'll need an outlet to process your emotions.

The support role you're assuming is not an easy one. In fact, being her ally in healing will affect you in ways you aren't prepared for. At times you'll feel alone and misunderstood. You may feel drained of energy, sad, and irritated. You'll long for a normal life.

Discouragement sometimes overcomes even the most determined men. At a weak moment, they succumb to the question, "Is it worth it?" They struggle to know, "Will she ever be whole? Is there a light at the end of the tunnel, and if so, how long is the tunnel?"

Positive self-talk and affirmations can help you in those times. Tell yourself, "Seeing her whole is worth the journey," or, "I give myself permission to be happy, even if she isn't there yet."

Talk to Someone

Your survivor probably isn't the person you should turn to with everything. Although you want to be honest with her, you must consider timing. When a woman's going through certain aspects of her healing, her emotional energy and focus are directed on her pain. She's looking to you for strength. So make sure you have at least one other person to turn to for support, objectivity, and accountability. It may be a pastor, professional counselor, or even a close friend, but talk to someone.

If Terry had found a safe place where he could have gone to vent and unload his frustrations, we may not have ended up a divorce statistic. But he kept his hurts to himself, and the wound festered.

It's important that you secure a good support person to confide in. Like Terry, most men don't find it easy to open up and share their deepest feelings, but this is one time you don't want to go it on your own. Talk about your anger. Unload your bewilderment and frustration. Reveal that you may feel inadequate and helpless. Helping a survivor is a daunting task, and we survivors let you know if we think you're not doing it right.

Her frequent irritation can leave you feeling uncertain of what to do or how to really help her. Talk about those insecurities. You're not betraying the one you love by finding someone to listen to you. But trust is a big issue with survivors, so if she feels threatened by your seeking outside help, you can simply say, "I love you and want to support you, but I can't do it alone." Or, "I want to remain supportive to you, so I'm making sure I'm taking care of my emotional needs, too."

Because you'll experience a gamut of emotions, finding someone you trust to express and explore them with will provide you with tremendous support and emotional relief. A safe sounding board will also give you some much-needed perspective.

Although you may tend to isolate yourself, staying open with your emotions and feelings will help you endure the journey and realize you're not alone. Other men have comforted survivors and lived to talk about it. You, too, can find your way through this maze.

Keep Healthy Personal Boundaries

Don't feel guilty if along the way you wonder, "Is it always just about her, or does she care that I have needs, too?" Discouragement comes to all of us when our personal needs are being neglected. So pay attention to what you're feeling. You have needs, too.

Keep your personal boundaries, and watch how much you take on. Avoid extremes. You can lose closeness with her by disconnecting from problems and ignoring her abuse issue or lose yourself by becoming overly involved. You can't fix her, so be careful not to try to solve her every problem.

Be honest about your needs. If it's appropriate timing, tell her what you're experiencing. "I'm feeling lonely and could use a hug from you." If she can handle physical touch, let her hug you, but be careful not to press her for more. Be trustworthy.

Face Your Anger

You've been walking around on tiptoes, trying not to rock her boat. But at times you want to scream, "What about me? Does anyone care about what I'm going through?"

You're the other victim. Her abusive past affects you in dramatic ways. You've been thrust into a support role you didn't try out for. Now you're standing stage left, second to her hurts and wounds.

It's not surprising that you feel angry. Most men in your situation do. Frustration, even rage at times, is to be expected.

Perhaps you've had to surrender some of your hopes and dreams in this relationship. Although most boys don't dream about their weddings like we women do, men do dream about the kind of women they will marry—women who will adore and fulfill them. That fulfillment can usually be summed up with two words: *sex* and *respect*.

Unfortunately, the two most frequent problems confronted by men married to survivors are sexual intimacy and respect. His dream of a satisfying relationship often turns into a nightmare.

Sex and respect are the two core issues related to abuse. In most cases, her abuser was a male, and a woman in survival often lumps all males in the same category and generalizes them all to be despicable and untrustworthy. She may be unaware that she feels this way, but her animosity toward men can run deep. After all, a man, through sexual abuse, stripped her of her most intimate and personal possession: her sexual dignity. A man with an abused partner is stripped, too. He's the second victim of sexual abuse. He's paying for the crime of another.

Just as she's learning to direct her anger at the right source and in the right manner, you, too, will need to learn to direct your anger in the right direction. You certainly want to rid yourself of the bitterness and resentment that may try to build, but finding constructive ways to release your anger is important. It's not necessary that you hide your feelings and emotions from her. Be honest about what you're feeling. But remember, she didn't choose this either.

Some types of anger are positive and appropriate. Anger can be the energy—the spinal fortitude—of healing. Identify the sources of your anger and work though them.

Men commonly experience the following sources of anger:

Over loss and change

Once she starts uncovering her destructive past, many things change. That change usually translates into loss for her husband.

+ Her moods change. She's no longer bubbly and outgoing, but sad and withdrawn.
+ Her sexual desires change. She isn't interested in sex or being close. She avoids kissing or touch.
+ Finances change. Counseling costs money. The energy it takes for her to hold a job is sucked away by sexual abuse.
+ Your relationship changes. It can deteriorate or become strained. You used to enjoy life together, but she isolates herself or has become unsocial.

At her abuser

"I feel cheated. He didn't only steal from you, he stole from me, too."

Terry was angry with my father, and he had a right to feel that way. He recognized that my dad had scarred me for life, and he had victimized Terry, too.

Maybe you've come to realize you're full of rage toward her abuser. Oftentimes, you both still have to deal with a family member. That was the case for us. Terry had to process his anger toward my dad, which was difficult for me. In a typical dysfunctional way, I defended my dad. "He didn't know what he was doing. He was drunk." Be careful with your anger toward her abuser. She may still be conflicted with her feelings toward her abuser.

Because she didn't tell you

You didn't sign up for this, and it's not what you expected. You're angry because she didn't tell you or warn you about her past. Maybe she mentioned it, but you had no idea what the ramifications would be, and neither did she. Many survivors deny the impact of their abuse. Only after being in a marriage relationship do they understand the horrendous ripple effect of sexual abuse.

Over powerlessness

"Nothing I do appears to be right. And nothing I say seems to help."

You feel helpless and useless. You're angry that you can't fix this. Many men are angry that they feel so completely out of control.

Take a Break

Your commitment to her is important to you; that's probably why you're reading this book. But the healing process can consume your life if you let it. In writing this book, I've been reminded of how intense the struggle of overcoming sexual abuse is. At times I've wanted to throw up my hands and say, "It's too emotional, I can't do it."

When you feel overwhelmed, you need to take a breather. And taking a break can be good for her, too. When stress and pressure escalate, it's okay to remove yourself from the intensity. I'm not suggesting you leave in an angry huff after an argument or in frustration. But when you're feeling stripped of your energy, let her know you need a "time-out." Take a day and go fishing or participate in whatever activity you enjoy. Giving yourself personal space and time can be therapeutic for both of you.

Survivors need a break from the healing process, too. Encourage her to give herself a day off from the mental grind of recovery. Once you've taken a reprieve, she can get back to working toward her healing.

Be Empowered

You have choices along the way. You're not trapped, you're committed. The decision to stay and fight through the devastation of sexual abuse is yours.

So live empowered as you travel beside your survivor. You can refuse to become the victim of sexual abuse by being informed about how the aftermath of assault is operating in your life, your marriage, and in the life of the woman you love.

Accept what you cannot change, and be courageous enough to change what you can. Identify and eliminate, as best you can, the crazy cycles that will undoubtedly try to take over your life.

Remember that "keeping peace at all cost" is not peace at all. Not for you, and ultimately not for her either. Acquiescing to the dysfunction of sexual abuse doesn't help the healing process. Instead, face circumstances with honesty; the woman you love is a survivor.

Her healing is an adventure, and you play a significant role. Your reward comes as you see her freed, day by day, as she steps into the life she was created to live.

31

QUESTIONS MEN HAVE

Helpers like you have many questions about the recovery process for sexual abuse survivors. It's not uncommon for men to feel "in over their heads" when it comes to abuse. One husband said, "I wish there was a playbook I could read so I knew what to do." You may nod your head in agreement. Healing isn't an exact science, and there are no hard, fast answers, yet there are some helpful insights I'd like to share to these common questions.

When will she heal?

Every survivor is different and her recovery unique. Her healing time is influenced by many factors. How severe was her abuse? How long did it last? Who was her abuser?

Recovery also depends on her current circumstances. What kind of support does she have now? Is she getting professional help? Is she in a safe and accepting environment?

Other factors in her healing journey include the kind of person she is, her temperament, and how she copes. How badly does she want to heal? How much time and energy does she have to devote to her recovery process? Is she determined to go the distance in inner healing?

The healing process is not linear. If you can think of it in terms of a winding path full of twists and turns, you'll have more reasonable expectations. The woman you love may start to relapse in an area you thought she previously conquered, or you may find you're revisiting a phase you thought she'd passed through. Don't be too alarmed; setbacks are part of the journey, and relapse is a part of recovery.

Her healing will take as long as it takes. There are no set timetables. More often than not, deep and lasting inner healing takes many months, if not years. This may sound like an eternity to you, but instant healings aren't rare; they're miraculous.

What if I suspect her abuse, but she hasn't told me yet?

Many survivors block out their sexual abuse experience. They have no memories, or their recollections are vague and incomplete. Yet the survivor's behavior can be perplexing and confusing and reveal that something terrible has happened to them. Other survivors deny being abused or greatly minimize the severity of it.

If you suspect your partner is a survivor but she hasn't told you yet, she may need you to help her talk about it. You can say things like, "I want you to know that nothing you can tell me will change my love for you." Or, "I'm here for you. Together we can face any trial." Your reassurance of love and support gives her courage to face the harsh realities of her sexual abuse.

She also needs your sensitivity to tell her story. Don't pry it out of her, but help her know you're prepared to love her through anything that comes your way. When she does finally break her silence and open up, you'll probably feel a sense of relief and grief at the same time. You've found the missing piece to the puzzle, and it all makes sense now. Her admission brings clarity to the picture you've been seeing. But you'll also grieve. The woman you love has been tragically violated.

Will she ever enjoy sex again?

Many women place a moratorium on sexual relations while working through their sexual assault. Since sex is associated with heartache and humiliation, the survivor tends to avoid it because sexual intimacy conjures up so many traumatic emotions. It's difficult for her to relax and surrender to pleasure when she must simultaneously battle negative and painful triggers.

But as she confronts the issues of her past and receives inner healing, her sexual desire may increase.

When her sexual drive returns, her ability to enjoy sex will greatly rest on your patience and understanding. The responsibility doesn't fully rest on you, but she must learn to reprogram her mind when it comes to sexual intimacy.

When did I become the enemy?

It wasn't fair. It wasn't even right, but it happened. My husband became the enemy. I didn't mean to make him the enemy, but many of the things he said and did seemed painfully familiar to me.

He was a man, for starters. And for a while, I was angry with all men.

He always wanted sex. And I did too, at first. But something happened to dampen my desire for intimacy. His approaches seemed intrusive and demanding, and I felt overpowered. He forced his touch on me. Now I know my aversion was, in part, because I had started the healing process, and I was triggered. I was relieved to find out I wasn't alone in my reaction. But the more he pressed me, the less of an ally he became. He went into enemy territory.

He kept important decisions from me. He wasn't up for spirited discussions (my terminology) or knock-down drag-out fights (his terminology) that were inherently part of our decision making. Therefore, he acted independently instead of being a team player.

It's not uncommon for survivors to treat men like the enemy. One day you may hear the words, "You men are all the same. None of you can be trusted."

That's when you'll know there's a chasm between you, and it needs to be bridged quickly.

On one hand, her anger is a sign that she's grasping the depth of the violation against her. She's finding her individuality and gaining a new identity. But on the other hand, her blanket generalizations are harmful if she doesn't learn how to separate you from her abuser.

What if she doesn't want help?

If a surviving woman is not ready to get help yet, you can't force her. In fact, if she feels pushed or manipulated, she'll likely dig in her heals even deeper and refuse your support or professional counseling.

But don't let her reluctance for help stop you. Express your honest feelings. Since a marriage partner is usually the closest person to a survivor, your observations, feelings, and opinions carry valuable weight. Share them with her.

You can tell her, "I notice you're struggling, honey, and I believe you'd benefit from having another person to talk to about your experience. I encourage you to seek a counselor. I'll go with you and support you any way I can." Then wait and let her progress to the point where she feels ready.

In the meantime, you may have to establish your boundaries as delicately as you can, but don't forsake them. Your healthy behavior can be a catalyst for her healing.

Many of your questions may have clear answers, but others may fall into the "every situation is unique" category. Asking questions about your survivor and sexual abuse is important. Your inquiries show you're engaged in her recovery and you want to be informed. As you learn, you gain greater power to help the woman you love overcome her past.

Continue to seek resources and counsel. Don't give up. Know that for every victory you see, she's fought a hundred unseen battles.

I challenge you to arm yourself and remain in the battle beside her.

— *32* —

FINDING PEACE

"Weeping may remain for a night, but rejoicing comes in the morning."
(Psalm 30:5)

"How long will it take before we find peace?"

Most men supporting an abuse survivor ask the same question. And the answer is always the same: it takes as long as it takes. Every woman is different. Her experiences are unique, her temperament distinctive. All these factors determine the healing progress.

One thing is certain, however. Your attitude toward her and the recovery process will either promote or hinder her healing. It's not fair to say it all rests on you. But because she was hurt in the context of human contact and relationship, it makes sense that her healing will be achieved the same way—through human contact and the interaction you share in your relationship. You can be God's instrument to show her love, compassion, trust, and intimacy.

As the man in her life you possess powerful influence.

Yet, statistics show that most—although not all—sexually abused women have been abused by a man, and that puts you in a precarious position. She can view you as another man in a long line of men that have hurt her, rejected her, and overpowered her if your actions are too aggressive. A man's demeanor, size, and even the sound of his voice can feel threatening to a woman.[1]

---

1. "Child Sexual Abuse," The United States Department of Veterans Affairs, Information on Trauma and PTSD, last modified December 20, 2011, http://www.ptsd .va.gov/public/pages/child-sexual-abuse.asp.

However, you can play a powerful healing role in her life. God can use you to show her how a man is supposed to love his partner. Through your patience and gentleness, she'll learn that a man's touch can be healing and comforting, not demanding and painful. You can help her see that yielding to you is not something to be afraid of, but wonderfully fulfilling.

By working together, you can find peace in the midst of the sexual abuse storm.

I wish that were my story. For me, peace would come another way.

✦   ✦   ✦

I sat abandoned on the end of the bed. The motel room in New Orleans could not have been more desolate. I was frozen again. My gaze was fixed on the dingy motel door for what felt like hours. I was certain Terry would return to the forsaken place he'd left me. If it weren't for the screaming sirens outside the window, the silence would have been excruciating.

Yet in the midst of my despair, I felt the Lord Jesus speak to my heart. "Weeping may last for a night, Dawn, but your joy will come in the morning."

I sensed that God was showing me that my marriage would end. I realized the sorrow, fear, and hurt I had been experiencing would culminate with gruesome finality: the death of my marriage was inevitable.

Divorce is always devastating. But after twenty-seven years of marriage, I can't begin to describe the anguish our separation caused. Now, several years later, I still can't help but feel my childhood sexual abuse was one of the root causes.

One day while writing about my past, I felt a surge of emotion. Hot tears streamed down my face. I could still feel the hurt of Terry's betrayal and abandonment.

He was a young man with big dreams. He wasn't a monster. Managing a wife who'd been sexually molested hadn't been his dream for his life.

But that's what he got: A wife with special needs. Wounded, hurting, defensive, and scared.

But I was also a survivor—emerging as a whole woman.

The more I thought about it, the more I wanted to know if Terry realized how badly I'd hurt over the years of our marriage. So I took a moment and emailed him. I was ready to hear his point of view. I needed to understand. The words poured out as I wrote:

> Did you know how deeply affected I was by sexual abuse?
>
> Did you know how delicate I was? How scared I was to be touched?
>
> Did you know I was suffering deeply inside and needed you to say to me once, "How can I help you? Let's do this together"?
>
> Do you know how it hurt me when you said, "You're damaged goods"?
>
> Or when you said, "I won't learn some damn combination"?
>
> Did you know how trust between us was broken?
>
> Did you know I wanted to heal but did it alone because I was embarrassed to let you in?
>
> Did you know my dad made me touch him?
>
> Did you know how afraid I was to touch you?
>
> Did you know I was sure I would touch you wrong?
>
> Did you know I wanted to learn how to love you right, but instead I just shut down? You wouldn't teach me, talk to me, or ask me.
>
> You didn't share anything out loud: "That feels good. I love it when you do that, touch me here," anything.
>
> Did you know I was ashamed to have a sexual drive because I felt bad, wrong, sinful?
>
> Did you know these things?
>
> How did my abuse past affect you?

A few minutes later, I received this response. "As I sit here today with tears in my eyes, looking back, I would do things so differently! But . . . give me time to try to respond!"

I waited a few days. I was fairly sure I'd never hear from Terry again. Then one day, his response came. It was open and honest:

Yes, Dawn,

I understood all that you write about.

We might not have had good communication about all of this, but there was understanding. I can remember many times trying to be gentle and trying to have something with you, but, Dawn, it just never would work. I felt your defense walls supported by more defense walls. I think we both just shut down, too young to really know how to surmount such a thing.

I wanted it to be good, but as hard as I think I tried, I could not take the rejection either. It's hard to explain, I guess as hard as it is, and how hurtful it is, after a while you just lose heart! You just don't care. I became a victim, too.

I can remember sitting in the sex counselor's office [I never knew he went] and talking and him saying to me, "You must really feel gypped." I remember I almost broke down. I wanted to cry, but I didn't. I can remember trying to talk about it. I never felt it would be received right.

I think for us and for me, with all the other things that were going on in my life, I got to the point where I just didn't have anything else to do but make some drastic change. You know me; I never really cared what people think. I know God knew my heart. Dawn, bottom line, I could never see it changing. I can't change people. I couldn't change you. I see the effects of abuse all over. I'm just not sure people ever get over the effects. Dawn, the sex was the problem in our marriage, but I know I lost your respect, too. You said it all the time: "Respect is earned." I couldn't do it. I couldn't get it! I could go on and on.

Dawn, listen to me! I'm so sorry. I hold nothing against you. I still think you are an amazing girl. I love you very much. In spite of it all.

I know you loved me. We both are guilty. I know I didn't do things real well. I think about it all, and it makes me know of the Grace. It gives me a discerning heart. You don't need to look far to see a hurting person. I'm sorry.

I read Terry's words with sadness. We both became victims of my brutal past.

✦   ✦   ✦

Today, almost forty years after my sexual abuse, I'm at peace. I've experienced healing at a deep level. I live in the present, no longer tormented by my past.

I'm free to explore God's marvelous potential for my life, and I look forward to each new day.

I've forgiven those who hurt me.

And I've been forgiven.

The dark and stormy night is over. Morning has come, and with it, great joy.

I'm free.

For a safe place where hurting women can connect with other survivors, you can direct the woman you love to my website, www .dawnjones.org, where they'll find a link to the blog, "Women Shattering the Silence."

— *Epilogue* —

I want to tell you the rest of the story.

I believe that God's a redeemer—he takes what Satan means for evil and uses it for his glory. But honestly, after my divorce I had my doubts, "God, how can you receive glory from sexual abuse?" "Where is your glory in divorce?" Still, I prayed that God would somehow take my mess, turn it around, and give me something beautiful.

Something beautiful breezed into my life like a gentle, fresh wind on a warm, spring day. Twenty months later, I married Paul Damon.

Many survivors question whether or not they will ever be capable of a healthy relationship. They wonder if intimacy will always be a problem, or if authentic trust will ever be a reality. Today, I hold out a beacon of hope to assure every survivor that yes, a healthy relationship is possible. Ultimately, God wants the marriage you are in to be that healthy, whole relationship.

My marriage to Paul is indeed beautiful and priceless. We enjoy freedom, openness, laughter, and trust. The issues of my past have dissolved into God's healing grace-waters. I'm truly free because of the cleansing and healing power of Jesus Christ.

God offers the same healing to you.

— Acknowledgments —

To my husband, Paul Damon. You are the love of my life, my soul mate. I love you with every fiber of my being.

To Cecil Murphey, who made this book possible. Cec, you're a fabulous mentor and teacher, and I sincerely thank you for drawing the deep things out of me.

To my editor, Steve Barclift, who believed in this book and took a chance on me.

To Shelly Beach for being an incredible networking genius. I love you, my friend.

To my family and friends who supported and loved me through the process. Jeff and Dina Hackert, Missy Lettinga, Cleo Elve, and Laurie Plummer. You mean the world to me.

Special thanks to my children: Lisa, Angela, and Tony. You are my reward.

— *About the Author* —

For over twenty years, God has used Dawn Scott Jones to touch people through her personal testimony, her humor, and her writing. Her work has been published in *Charisma*, *Light and Life*, *SpiritLed Woman*, *Power Up*, as well as Zondervan's *Grandmother's Bible*. She is a national speaker who has been featured at national conferences, such as *Time Out for Women*, as well as *Women of Worth*. Dawn's past challenges have deepened and enriched her ministry, enabling her to understand and relate to others. Many hurting people have received healing through Dawn's teaching and story of inner healing.

Dawn is an ordained minister and has served in a variety of capacities including executive pastor in churches in the Midwest. She and her husband, Paul, reside in the Grand Rapids, Michigan, area.

For more information on Dawn Scott Jones, visit her website at www.dawnjones.org.